To Evangelos S., the mentor's mentor, who nurtured my interest in the language arts from the womb.

RJK

To all of the young men at the Hyde School in the late sixties and to Sumner Hawley, who taught me the importance and reward of teaching adolescents to write well, this is a small payment on a large debt.

JC

I want to thank my colleagues, Bob and Jim, for investing valuable time in such an extensive project. It has been a pleasure to work with both of you.

LD

CONTENTS

TABLES

PREFACE

TO RESEARCHERS AND LANGUAGE-ARTS PRACTITIONERS

The process of composing text involves a complex set of interactions. The writer interacts not only with the composed text but also with the semantic and episodic knowledge of text (i.e. schemas) as well as the subject matter, context, and meaning of text existing in her memory. The research work and instructional materials presented in this book are based on an interactive model of the reading process developed by Ruddell and Speaker (1985). Researchers who read this book will be interested in the hypotheses derived from a cognitive view of the reading and writing processes along with the noteworthy conclusions of our research. Those interested in the effects of a sentence-combining approach on students' writing should note how the conclusions of this study differ from those proffered by John Mellon. This book should also interest researchers who seek evidence that syntax might function in precise ways as a cognitive organizer, or that each syntactic structure might host a certain range of cognitive structures. Finally, our research provides some empirical evidence that Pitkin's (1977a, 1977b) ideas of discourse function can, indeed, be applied successfully to sentence-combining pedagogy.

Curriculum supervisors and language arts teachers might find Chapter 6 helpful in a number of ways. First, focusing the cognitive viewpoint more narrowly, it presents what might be called a behavioral model of how a complex behavior, like expository writing, can be shaped *gradually* through a series of connected activities. These activities, some of which can become amusing word games, are easily implemented and easily assimilated by students. Secondly, these lessons collectively illustrate one effective approach to the contextualization of learning in the language arts, which is currently a critical issue in the context of local, state, and national reform agenda. In this case, a ninth-grade biology text was used as the content source for all of the writing instruction. Finally, these lessons model one strategy for bringing traditional grammar instruction out of isolation, integrating syntax and writing instruction in a manner that demonstrates significant posttest growth in both areas.

One word of warning to practitioners who would adopt this approach in the hope of enhancing students' written performance. The many significant effects documented in our research resulted from eight consecutive weeks of instruction. (See *Design and Treatment* in Chapter 3.) The authors cannot predict how modifying the treatment, in any degree, might alter the effects observed in the present study.

ACKNOWLEDGMENTS

High schools are busy places, particularly in Massachusetts where systems are scurrying to align themselves with learning standards promulgated by recent educational reform. We gratefully acknowledge the administration at the experimental site -- in particular Charlie Lyons, Bob Cunningham, and John Judge -- who found time to enthusiastically support our study during this energetic transition. Special thanks also to the teachers who counted words, clauses, and T-units and rated the quality of essays. These are tasks reserved for only the most tenacious, who in our study included Ralph Carvalho, Bill Jansen, Leah Marquis, Margarida Mello, Gail Poulten, and Bob Sheehy. Finally, our gratitude to Donna DiFranco for her patient assistance.

CHAPTER 1

AN OVERVIEW

Introduction

Although composition classrooms in schools and college commonly provide direct instructions in traditional grammar, research on the teaching of syntax has fallen upon hard times. Shortly after Braddock et al (1963) argued that grammar instruction is more likely to do more harm than good as an instructional focus, Thibodeau (1964) concluded that a brief 6-week grammar treatment has a negative effect on sixth graders' writing. Later, a much longer 96-week grammar treatment produced no significant differences in the overall writing quality of eleventh graders (Elley at al, 1976). More recently, Hillocks' (1986) meta-analysis of grammar treatments supported Braddock's contention. Hillocks' data showed that students in grammar and mechanics treatments scored .29 standard deviation less than their peers in treatments excluding those objectives. Hillocks concluded that, in comparison to grammar treatments, "nearly anything else is more effective in increasing the quality of writing (214)."

The grammar treatments investigated in these studies focused exclusively on the study of the parts of speech and their usage in sentences. In this context, grammar instruction is an element in a bottom-up (essentially behaviorist) approach to writing. Such an approach begins with the study of words and their parts then introduces progressively longer and more complex chunks of text including phrases, clauses, sentences, and paragraphs. This traditional focus, however, is not the exclusive approach to grammar instruction. In 1969, Mellon pioneered a syntactic treatment known as transformational sentence combining which changed not only the traditional activity but also the empirical outcome associated with grammar instruction.

As introduced by Mellon, sentence combining activity encourages students to write longer, more complex sentences in exercises which signal or cue syntactic strategies for joining simple base clauses. The technique is uncomplicated and easily taught, and the cued activity is essentially a cognitive view of writing which reflects Neisser's (1969) analysis-by-synthesis feature detection theory of perception and the influence of perception on comprehension and performance. Beginning with O'Hare (1973), a series of experiments curiously but repeatedly demonstrated that sentence-combining treatments could significantly enhance measures of overall writing quality (Combs, 1975; Schuster, 1976; Pedersen, 1977; Waterfall, 1977; Swan, 1977, and Kerek et al, 1980.) Hillocks' (1986) meta-analysis of sentence-combining studies concluded that the effect size of those treatments is significantly greater than that of traditional grammar studies that he investigated.

A great debate about these findings ensued but essentially remained unresolved. No one working in the writing area discovered the casual link between sentence-combining treatments and enhanced measures of overall writing quality. In her review of the literature, Stotsky (1975) noted that sentence-combining programs seem to have been conducted "in a contextual vacuum (61)." But Kerek et al (1980) insist that a careful reading of the literature suggests the opposite, and these investigators speculate that the language experience acquired through sentence-combining practice enables students to turn out better papers because "the experimental classes extensively discussed commonly included contextual considerations (106)."

Our research explored precisely that assumption. That is, contextualization of syntactic activity can be linked to enhance measures of overall writing quality. Our research investigated the effects of sentence-combining activity that promotes reading, thinking, and writing in specific rhetorical contexts. Our treatment consisted of a series of sentence-combining units each of which models syntactic strategies for developing one discourse purpose (or function) like comparison, contrast, or cause and effect. Our treatment has thus been called "discourse-function sentence-combining." The discourse functions modeled in the treatment are borrowed from Pitkin (1977b), who has for some time urged writing teachers to demonstrate to their students just how "discourse function determines, or at least should determine, [syntactic] choices (654)."

Purpose

The purpose of our research was to investigate the effects of a discourse-function sentence-combining treatment on the written syntactic maturity and overall quality of the expository writing of ninth graders.

The major benefit of our research is that it contributed to knowledge pertaining to those sentence-combining treatments which are designed to enhance measures of overall writing quality. The support of most of the major hypotheses suggests that one explanation for sentence-combining's effectiveness as a writing treatment is the application of Pitkin's principles of discourse hierarchy. Empirical support of our major hypotheses will also indicate that a more cognitive view of the writing process, and of the process of learning to write, is needed.

Our research should be of particular interest to English teachers seeking a new approach to instruction in syntax as well as to curriculum writers seeking a new method of integrating language, writing, and content-area objectives.

Research Questions

The following research questions both guided and were the focus of our research efforts:

1. How will a discourse-function sentence-combining treatment affect measures of subjects' syntactic maturity in expository writing?
2. How will a discourse-function sentence-combining treatment affect measures of subjects' overall expository writing quality?
3. How will a discourse-function sentence-combining treatment affect the quality of subjects' main idea in expository writing?
4. How will a discourse-function sentence-combining treatment affect the quantity and quality of subjects' details in expository writing?

5. How will a discourse-function sentence-combining treatment affect the organization of subjects' expository compositions?
6. How will a discourse-function sentence-combining treatment affect the cohesion of subjects' expository compositions?
7. How will a discourse-function sentence-combining treatment affect sentence structures in subjects' expository writing?
8. How will a discourse-function sentence-combining treatment affect the quality of usage in subjects' expository writing?

These research questions created the following working hypotheses:

1. The <u>syntactic maturity</u> of expository compositions written by the experimental subjects will be significantly higher than those written by the control subjects.
2. The experimental subjects will write expository compositions that will be judged significantly superior in <u>overall quality</u> than expository compositions written by control subjects.
3. The <u>main ideas</u> in the expository compositions written by the experimental subjects will be judged significantly more clearly expressed than those written by the control subjects.
4. The <u>details</u> that support main idea in the expository compositions written by the experimental subjects will be judged significantly more relevant to the main ideas and more sufficient in number than those written by the control subjects.
5. The global <u>organization</u> of the expository compositions written by the experimental subjects will be judged significantly more orderly and logical than that of the expository compositions written by the control subjects.
6. The local <u>cohesion</u> between adjoining sentences of the expository composition written by the experimental subjects will be judged significantly more connected than that of the expository compositions written by the control subjects.
7. The <u>sentence structure</u> of the expository compositions written by the experimental subjects will be judged significantly more varied than that of the expository compositions written by the control subjects.
8. The <u>usage</u> in the expository compositions written by the experimental students will be judged significantly more concise and significantly more consistent with the conventions of Standard

English than that of the expository compositions written by the control subjects.

We also investigated several other hypotheses, derived from the preceding working hypotheses, that will be discussed in subsequent chapters.

Definition of terms

Due to the plethora of concepts and specialized terms that are used in the literature on writing and discourse function, key concepts and terms are defined below so that the reader may be introduced to the specialized vocabulary and may know the operational definitions of the terms that we employed in our research. We are well aware that this list of key concepts and terms is rather long, but it must be so, given the nature of our research topic and the controversy that surrounds this topic.

Absolute. A phrase that stands apart from the normal syntax of the sentence, much like a close-up shot in film. For example: The professor jotted notes on the blackboard before class, the billowing clouds of smoke form his pipe concealing him amid his thoughts.

Anaphora. The use of a word as a substitute for a preceding word or group of words; backward reference as it in The hurricane winds soon downed many trees, and it got worse by the hour.

Automaticity. Response or behavior without attention or conscious effort. Automaticity in word attack permits full energy to be used in developing comprehension.

Base clause. See "main clause."

Causal inference. An inference that establishes a cause-and-effect link between two propositions in text.

Chunking. The process in which informational items arriving in short-term memory are organized into a single unit based on relationships that are detected among the items. The information can range from individual letters to ideas expressed in text.

Clause. Any group of words that contains a subject and a verb. An independent (or main) clause states complete meaning. A dependent clause states incomplete meaning.

Cohesion.   The linkage of ideas within or between sentences.   Irwin
   (1986) distinguishes cohesion, which she calls "local
   connectedness," from organization, which she calls "global
   connectedness."
Coordinate idea.   In Christensen's program, an idea that details or
   modifies a referent at the same level of generality as another
   modifier. For example:
   1.   The lonely student scanned the dusty stack,
   2.   straining his eyes at the worn binding,
   2.   hoping to find the obscure volume, but
   2.   sensing that his evening would end in disappointment.
        The consecutive participial phrases, each of which is
        numbered 2, are coordinate ideas in this sentence. Because
        each phrase details the base clause at the same level of
        semantic generality, Christensen calls the phrases coordinate
        ideas.
Coreference cue.   Textual information that refers to and establishes the
   identity of one subject between or among sentences.   Such
   information frequently varies lexically and syntactically.
Cumulative sentence.   A sentence which ends with at least one final free
   modifier.   Christensen's approach emphasized participial,
   absolute, appositive, and prepositional phrases as final, free
   modifiers.
Discourse-function sentence combining.   Sentence-combining activity
   whose lessons are organized around rhetorical operations (e.g.
   comparison, contrast, cause-and-effect), with various syntactic
   structures subgrouped under them.
Ellipsis.   The omission of part of a sentence that is not necessary for
   meaning. For example, in the sentence Carol's baccalaureate is
   from Lowell State College , and mine is too, the words from
   Lowell State College are clearly understood in the meaning of the
   second clause and thus elliptically omitted.
Embedded structure.   A restrictive or nonrestrictive structure contained
   within a main clause. For example: Whatever he said placated
   the board members (restrictive noun clause).   The student,
   smiling broadly from one end of his keyboard to the other,
   concluded the draft of his proposal (nonrestrictive participial
   phrase.) See "restrictive" and "nonrestrictive structures."

Episodic knowledge. Knowledge associated with specific events that happened once at a given time. Episodic knowledge is stored in episodic memory.

Expository writing. A mode of writing that organizes information within text in order to define, compare, contrast, or in some way analyze the idea. Although expository writing can include limited amounts of narration, description, and argument, its primary purpose of setting forth or explaining information sets it apart f-om the other rhetorical modes.

Final free modifier. Nonrestrictive elements that are attached to the end of a main clause. See "cumulative sentence."

Functional hierarchy. The analysis or organization of text in terms of stages and substages of one rhetorical operation (e.g. comparison, contrast, cause and effect.) (Pitkin, 1977 a, b)

Generative rhetoric. A method developed by Christensen (1986) which attempts to increase written syntactic fluency by controlled writing practice. Students are required to supply content and manipulate syntactic structures in order to produce (1) cumulative sentence and (2) paragraphs structured according to the principles of Christensen's semantic hierarchy.

Lexical knowledge. The denotative or "dictionary" meaning of a word stored in semantic memory.

Macrostructure. The global or most general structure of text. The disclosure purpose establishes the most general "shape" of the macrostructure. See "Mode of discourse."

Main clause. The independent clause to which subordinate elements are joined in a sentence. The main clause is sometimes called the base clause of a sentence. Compound sentences contain more than one main clause.

Microstructure. The propositions and their syntactic environments, the sentences, and the sequences of sentences which make up text.

Minimal terminable unit. One main clause and any subordinate clause or nonclausal structure attached to or embedded in it. (Hunt, 1965.)

Mode of discourse. One of four types or classifications of discourse purpose which include description, narration, exposition, and argument.

Need to infer. The awareness of a reader that some type of relationship (e.g. cause and effect) must link or resolve two propositions in text. (Ackerman, 1986)

Nonrestrictive structure. Phrases or dependent clauses that add details not essential to the meaning of the main clause. For example: The young child pronounced every word correctly, beaming proudly as she sat among her classmate. Because the final participial phrase is not essential to the meaning of the main clause, it is considered nonrestrictive, and it is set-off form the main clause by a comma. See "restrictive structure."

Parallel structures. Similar syntactic structures which perform similar syntactic functions in or between sentences. For example: To err is human, to forgive divine. The subject of both clauses, expressed as infinitives, are parallel structures.

Parallelism. The use or presence of parallel structure in text. See "parallel structures."

Restrictive structure. Phrases or dependent clauses that add essential detail to the meaning of the main clause. For example: The young child who pronounced every word correctly is my daughter. Because the underlined adjective clause is essential to the meaning of the main clause, the adjective clause is restrictive, and it is not set-off from the rest of the sentence by commas. See "nonrestrictive structures."

Semantic hierarchy. The analysis or organization of text in terms of stages and substages of semantic generalization. (Christensen, 1963, 1965, 1967)

Semantic knowledge. General knowledge which (1) cannot be traced to a single event and (2) seems to be the abstraction of common elements from variety of previous episodes. Semantic knowledge is stored in semantic memory.

Sentence combining. writing instruction that requires the student (1) to rewrite independent clauses as dependent clauses and nonclauses and (2) to join those rewritten structures to other clauses and elements for the purpose of creating a prose style characteristic of experienced writers. "Cued" exercises prescribe specific ways to combine syntactic structures. "Open" exercises contain no cues and leave combination strategies to the student's option.

Subordinate idea. In Christensen's program, an idea at a lower level of generality (i.e., a more detailed idea) than the idea that it is modifying or detailing. This distinction between main and subordinate ideas is semantic, not syntactic. The following sentence, by Sinclair Lewis, illustrates a subordinate sequence:

    1. He dipped his hand in the bichloride solution and shook
       them,
      2. a quick shake,
        3. fingers down,
          4. like the fingers of a pianist above the keys.
The main or base clause is numbered 1. The final free modifiers
numbered 2, 3, and 4 descend into progressively lower levels of
generality and are therefore subordinate ideas to Christensen.
See "Coordinate idea."

Syntax. The pattern or structure of word order in phrases, clauses, or
    sentences.

Syntactic fluency. A measure of the observable range of sentence types
    employed by the writer (Mellon, 1969.)
    A measure of the observable range of sentence types employed
    by the writer (Mellon, 1969.)

Syntactic maturity. A measure of a writer's growth according to indices
    compiled by Hunt (1965) which identify mean values of five
    syntactic variables at three grade levels (4, 8 and 12) and for
    skilled adults. The syntactic variables include: words per clause,
    clauses per T-unit, words per T-unit, T-unit per sentence, and
    words per sentence.

Text structure. The hierarchal organization of text, i.e. the manner in
    which propositions are networked within the text to create a
    story or achieve some rhetorical purpose.

T-unit. See "minimal terminable unit."

Other concepts and terms will be introduced and defined in subsequent
chapters, but those introduced and defined here should help the reader
understand the theoretical background and methodology of our research
efforts.

Theoretical Background

    Language comprehension and production rely on the interaction of
different types of semantic knowledge and processes (See van Dijk and
Kintsch, 1983; Chomsky, 1985; and Westphal, 1991). . According to
the interactive model of Ruddell and Speaker (1985), a language user
comprehends text and produces written responses to it by activating
Decoding, Language, and World Knowledge. These subcomponents

comprise the universe of Declarative and Procedural Knowledge within the model (See Anderson, 1985). Declarative knowledge is all semantic information about decoding, language, and the world stored in memory. Procedural knowledge is the language user's store of semantic strategies necessary for processing text. The most generalized model of this cognitive or information processing model of learning and performance has been outlined by Carifio (1993) and Dagostino and Carifio (1994). The reader is referred to these for greater explication of the general model.

The reader's decoding knowledge allows him to recognize letters and words, the most rudimentary visual textual information. The beginning language user chunks letters visually and phonetically in both isolation and simple contexts to derive simple meaning (LaBerge and Samuels, 1976.) Written output is enhanced as the language user gains proficiency in composing progressively larger chunks of modeled text. As the chunking process becomes increasing automatic, attention is freed for solving more complicated language tasks.

These more complicated tasks require Language Knowledge, which Ruddell and Speaker (1985) describe as a store of lexical, syntactic, and text-structure information. Basic to this construct is lexical knowledge-- the knowledge of vocabulary and word meanings. Davis (1972) concluded that, in study after study, lexical knowledge emerges as the most important factor in comprehension. Goodman (1980) and later Graves (1984) classified all new vocabulary encountered by the language user into four types, according to the type of prior knowledge a learner can activate to understand the words. They concluded that the comprehension of new word meanings is most difficult when words label complex concepts or when the words represent ideas for which synonymous meaning cannot be accessed in semantic memory.

Within the Language Knowledge component of the Ruddell and Speaker model, the hierarchy of semantic knowledge ascends from lexical to syntactic information. Not only must the reader be able to recognize syntactic structures, but he must also understand the relationship of words and structures within, between, or among sentences. Stotsky (1975) was among the earliest to assert that enhanced syntactic knowledge improved reading comprehension. Ackerman (1986) studied the relationship of the reader's recognition of syntactic coreference cues in text and his ability to establish a "need" for causal inferences.

Syntactic knowledge is also important to the writer, who must rely on this store of semantic information to create and combine chunks of text. In 1965, Hunt devised the "minimal terminable unit" ("T-unit," for short) to operationalize a construct that he called the writer's "syntactic maturity." Since that time, much attention has been paid to Hunt's measure, which is defined as one main clause and any subordinate clause or nonclausal structure attached to or embedded within it. In particular, investigators have been interested by the differential effects of text structure on written syntactic structures. Text-structure knowledge is the third and final component of the Ruddell and Speaker (1985) Language construct.

Ruddell and Speaker observe that the developing reader gradually becomes familiar with narrative and expository forms of written text as a result of his exposure to models that he encounters in his reading experience. On the most global level, the reader learns that the elements that give narrative text its structure include: characters, setting, problems and goals, episodes, and attempts to resolve the problems. In addition, the reader understands that expository text can structure information in different patterns like: cause and effect, comparison and contrast, description, and problem and solution.

This global text-structure information forms the semantic models used not only by the reader to comprehend text but also by the writer in the production of a parallel structures. (Ruddell and Speaker, p. 779.) It is beneath this global level of text knowledge that the differential interactions between text structure and syntax occur. For example, in the analysis of fourth-graders' composition, Martinez San Jose (1973) found that argument and exposition produced much longer and more complex T-units than narration and description. Crowhurst and Piche (1979) found that the T-unit length and clauses per T-unit of sixth- and tenth-grade writers were significantly greater for argument than for either narration or description. Curiously, however, there were no significant differences among the syntactic measures for narratives written at these two grade levels, suggesting that level of complexity might be an important factor.

Using an analytic instrument comprising seventeen syntactic variables, Watson (1980) found the persuasive writing of twelfth graders and upper-level college English majors significantly more complex than their expressive writing. Hennig (1980) found that the formal essays of college freshmen was significantly more complex than their personalized letters and journals on several indices of syntactic maturity. Nietzke (1972) found that the mean T-unit length of critical essays written by college freshman was significantly greater than the mean T-unit length of their personal experience writing.

Crowhurst (1980) examined syntactic differences of two modes of student compositions independently rated according to a quality scale. He computed the mean T-length unit for argument and narration written by sixth, tenth, and twelfth graders. Pairs of compositions by the same writer were selected for evaluation if one composition was of high complexity (at least .5 word greater than the mean for discourse mode and grade level) and the other composition was of low complexity (at least .5 word below the same mean.) Two rating scales were used, a 7-point holistic scale and a 7-category analytic instrument. Among sixth graders, no significant difference was discovered between high- and low-complexity narratives and arguments. Among tenth graders, no significant difference was discovered between low- and high-complexity narratives.

However, high-complexity arguments were rated significantly better than low-complexity arguments for both tenth (analytic measure only) and twelfth graders (both holistic and analytic measures.) And among twelfth graders low-complexity narratives were rated significantly better than high-complexity narratives on both measures. Crowhurst concluded that argument may demand "logical interrelationship of propositions" (p. 230) which requires, in turn, longer T-units. At any rate, Crowhurst's study strongly suggests the differentiated qualitative effects of text structure on syntax. Crowhurst's results were supported, in part, by Nold and Freedman (1977) and Faigley (1979) who found, by using stepwise multiple regression, that the two most important variables associated with the quality of expository composition were length and percent of T-units with final free modifiers. Other studies (Jurgens and Griffin, 1970; Martinez San Jose, 1973; Belanger, 1978; Stewart and Grobe, 1979) found no significant correlations between syntactic measure and assessments of overall quality.

In the broadest analysis, these investigations of the relationships between syntactic complexity, text structure and rated quality measure and evaluate interactions between microstructures and macrostructures in composing process (See van Dijk and Kintsch, 1983 and Westphal, 1991 for details). The smallest chunks of text comprise its microstructure; these chunks include phrases, clauses, sentences, and sequences of sentences which collectively express individual propositions. The macrostructure is the global, semantic network that links the individual propositions. While the preceding studies suggest that the two structural levels interact in some way during writing, they do not suggest how those interactions might be instructionally exploited to enhance the composition process and its products. Frederiksen (1987), however, provides one strategy. In his observation of students experiencing difficulty in the production of cohesive expository text, he noted that those writers were able to manipulate sentence structures, but not in a way related to the function and organization of the macrostructure. Frederiksen explains that, although students apparently do perceive sentence structures as objects that can be manipulated, they fail likewise to perceive the macrostructure design or purpose as a manipulatable object.

As a result, Frederiksen (1987, p. 9) proposed three types of instructional environments for planning and analyzing semantic structures in writing. In each of these environments, semantic text structures are represented graphically as objects on computer screens. In one environment, the text is analyzed or parsed in terms of its macrostructure and constituent propositions. In a second environment, these macrostructures are revised to suit varying expository designs. In a third environment (which Frederiksen calls the "semantic workbench"), original macrostructures are developed from the preceding models. Although Frederiksen pays some attention to the analysis of the propositional level of text in the respective environments, his proposed approach is decidely top-down, that is the instructional focus is the semantic macrostructure of text, and all other propositional and syntactic elements are viewed in relationship to it.

Williams (1989) observes that top-down strategies like that of Frederiksen represent the mainstream of current composition pedagogy and theory. If Williams is correct, "[w]riting, like reading, has come to be viewed as primarily a top-down process rather than bottom-up" (129). Williams insists that the range of syntactic, sentence-writing operations that can be performed in a bottom-up approach is limited and easily identifiable. He further argues that content, meaning, and purpose are too often ignored in a bottom-up approach. Williams criticizes Christensen (1967) and others who maintain that that increasing syntactic knowledge and fluency can effect global writing skills. "To date," concludes Williams (1989), "there is no solid evidence to support the idea that teaching students to write better sentences will lead to their writing a better essay" (130).

Notwithstanding Williams' conclusions, there exists some evidence that a sentence-level, syntactic approach to composition can significantly enhance measures of overall writing quality. Such gains have been shown in experimental subjects to whom sentence-combining treatments were administered in grade seven (Schuster, 1977; Pedersen, 1977; Combs, 1975; O'Hare, 1971) and in college (Kerek, Daiker, and Morenberg, 1980; Waterfall, 1977; Swan, 1977.) In deference to Williams, it must be noted that those studies tend to raise more questions than they answer. As Faigley (1979) observed:

> In spite of the collective successes of sentence-combining experiments, much about sentence combining remains to be understood. Little is known about what is essential for sentence-combining practice to work, what accounts for its effect, ...and how gains in syntactic maturity affect overall writing quality. (196)

Faigley added that researchers' ignorance associated with the outcomes of sentence-combining experiments likely stems from their lack of familiarity with other methods of writing instruction analagous to sentence combining. He then noted that an approach developed by Christensen (1967) called generative rhetoric paralleled sentence combining, and that to understand the former is to gain some insight into the effects of the latter. Faigley's comparison of the two approaches is reasonable.

Sentence-combining instruction requires the student (1) to transform independent clauses to dependent clauses and nonclauses and (2) to join them to other clauses and elements for the purpose of creating structures and writing styles characteristic of experienced writers. "Cued" sentence-combining exercises prescribe specific transformations through a system of signals or cues. The intended product of the cued exercise is a single, complexly structured sentence. "Open" sentence-combining exercises contain no cues. They comprise passages of syntactically simple and redundant but rhetorically related propositions which the writer is invited to combine in any appropriate manner. The intended product of the exercise is cohesive text which is syntactically more complex than the original passage.

Similarly, Christensen's generative-rhetoric approach requires students to manipulate syntactic structures to produce maturer writing. The most obvious dissimilarity between generative-rhetoric and sentence-combining activity is that the former requires the student to produce his own content. However, like proponents of the cued sentence-combining approach, Christensen paid much attention to syntactic structures within the sentence. The sentence-level objective of his generative rhetoric was the "cumulative sentence," which he steadfastly maintained characterized the style of professional writers and which he defined as a base clause and attached or embedded nonrestrictive modifiers. And like proponents of the open sentence-combined approach, Christensen paid much attention to the production of cohesive passage. He believed that the paragraph was another form of cumulative thought, and he advanced the idea that the base clause of a sentence and the topic sentence of a paragraph served analogous functions.

Despite their similarities, generative-rhetoric and sentence-combining activity have rarely emerged as combined elements of a singular approach to writing instruction. Strong (1973) devoted approximately one-third of Sentence Combining: A Composing Book, the text used by Kerek et al. (1980) in their Miami University experiment, to activity related to nonrestrictive sentence elements. Landwehr (1980) combined generative rhetoric and sentence combining in writing instruction to college freshmen. Towns (1984) suggested the appropriateness of such a combined approach to integrate reading and writing instruction in both secondary and post-secondary reading programs. And Broadhead and Berlin (1984) devised "Twelve Steps to Using Generative Sentences and Sentence Combining in the Composition Classroom." However, it appears that the constraints imposed by Christensen on his rhetoric of the sentence have, for the most part, turned sentence-combining researchers away from his technique.

Christensen insisted that the typical sentence written by a skilled adult contains, at or close to its beginning, a base clause. According to his principle of "addition," that base or main idea is then elaborated by one or more attached, nonrestrictive elements. Most commonly, Christensen observed, these elements were phrases like appositives, absolutes, participial phrases, and prepositional phrases. He dubbed this right-branching syntactic pattern the "cumulative sentence." Christensen's second principle, "direction of movement" held that such addition of nonrestrictive phrases tends to restate or in some way qualify the introductory mail clause. His third principle, "levels of generality" argues that in qualifying the main clause, the nonrestrictive elements progressively narrow the focus of the main idea until clearly detailed meaning emerges. In advancing his fourth and final principle, "texture," Christensen argued that sentences comprising many nonrestrictive elements (i.e. highly textured sentences) are qualitatively superior to sentences written in a plainer style.

Christensen's critics do not support the notion that the cumulative sentence is an exemplar of the style of skilled adult writers. Johnson (1969) opposes the exclusion of embedded clauses in Christensen's rhetoric. Mellon (1980) takes similar exception and, in marked contrast, pays much attention to embedded noun clauses as indicators of "syntactic fluency" in expository writing. Walker (1970) argues that the criteria for judging effective sentence writing far exceeds the presence or absence of final, nonrestrictive elements. Instead, Walker suggests that attention should be paid to developing parallel structures within and between the sentences of young writers.

Winterowd (1975) objects to Christensen's emphasis of only six types of nonrestrictive phrases and suggests that such instruction ignores many other syntactic structures commonly used by skilled writers. Tibbets (1970) accuses Christensen of the "fiction fallacy," "charging that the prose style nurtured by Christensen's rhetoric is more akin to that of fiction than of nonfiction. Becker (1965) claimed that Christensen's generative view of paragraph structure could not explain, in semantic terms, the network of coordinate and subordinate ideas within the paragraph. And Rodgers (1966) criticized Christensen's emphasis on the paragraph as the basic unit of discourse, proposing instead (sometimes larger) units that he called "stadia of discourse."

Despite this focused disagreement with sentence and paragraph structure in expository writing, the merit of Christensen's broader assumption has not been ignored. He believed that, at various structural levels of discourse, "Solving the problem of 'how to say' helps solve the problems of 'what to say' " (1968, vi). Christensen proposed that students could invent or generate a network of text structure and content by extrapolating a much smaller but central idea. Grady (1971) agreed that the body of an expository essay presents information at a level of generality lower than that of the introduction at a level of generality lower than that of the introduction--analogous to the structure of elements within the cumulative sentence. Similarly,

D'Angelo (1974) analyzed the structure of large chunks of text in terms resembling the cumulative sentence.

Pitkin (1977a) was a student of Christensen's at the University of Southern California and describes his admiration for his mentor as "boundless (655)." Nevertheless, Pitkin criticizes Christensen's hierarchal model of semantic generality in the strongest terms. Pitkin argues that his exception to the notion of a semantic hierarchy of discourse is supported by disclaimers issued by Christensen (1965) himself, who conceded that "When sentences are added to develop a topic or subtopic, they are usually at the lower end of generality, usually, but not always...(145)." Pitkin (1977a) points to subsequent notes--addended by Christensen (1967) to reprintings of both "A Generative Rhetoric of the Paragraph" and "A Generative Rhetoric of the Sentence"--which also disclaim that same position.

Despite all this disagreement, Pitkin (1977a, b), like Christensen, argued the merits of a hierarchal model of discourse, but the Pitkin model comprised successive levels of functional, not semantic, inclusiveness. Pitkin (1977a) reasoned that "Discourse does not occur within the individual base clause; it occurs only when base clauses are combined. 'Ben was hungry' is not discourse. 'Ben was hungry, so he fixed himself a sandwich is discourse.' (651)" Pitkin insists that such an utterance cannot be comprehended in terms of Christensen's semantic model. He observes that a general/specific, additive relationship between elements--the very foundation of the semantic model--is nowhere to be found in the utterance. Pitkin argues that most discourse similarly contradicts Christensen's logic. Instead, he explains, one decodes discourse by understanding the specific function (in the "Ben" utterance, a cause-and-effect operation) derived from combining bases.

In Pitkin's model, coherent discourse originates at a main stage with a binary operation that joins two propositions for the purpose of establishing a specific discourse strategy or function. The main stage comprises binary substages, each of which expands a main-stage proposition. The model can flow through subsequent substages which, according to Pitkin (1977a), are discernible on the basis of their discourse functions, not their syntactic forms. He assumes that the set of binary functions is finite--in fact, few in number. He stops just short of asserting that they are universal. Pitkin (1977a) lists and discusses those binary functions in "not a definitive taxonomy but a tentative catalog" which include:

1. Coordinate/Coordinate (e.g., x/and y).
2. Includer/Included (e.g., x/for example y)
3. Cause/Effect (e.g., because x/y).
4. Contrast/Contrast (e.g., not x/rather y)
5. Comparison/Comparison (e.g., like x/y)
6. Assertion/Intensification (e.g., x/indeed y).
7. Assertion/Regression (e.g., x/at least y).

The catalog concludes with three binary relationships which overlap the preceding seven:

8. Manner (Evaluation)/Assertion.
9. Time (Place)/Assertion.
10. Assertion/ Significance.

In the writing classroom, the binary characteristic of each discourse function quite naturally invites a sentence-combining approach, instruction which for many years has modeled strategies for the combination of (at least) "x" and "y" propositions. The unique modification of a sentence-combining approach based on Pitkin's operational model is the design of ten instructional units patterned after the preceding catalog. Each unit would model syntactic options for achieving a singular operation. Such an approach might aptly be called discourse-function sentence combining. Pitkin (1978) himself proposed such an idea, which he viewed as an opportunity for the student to compose (and the teacher to evaluate) text directed to very specific principles of logic, organization, and punctuation.

In "Sentence Manipulation and Cognitive Processes, "Suhor (1978) enthusiastically calls for such an approach to composition. Suhor argues that since sentence-combining activity enhances non-syntactic variables like ideas and quality of diction, investigators should become interested in discovering the connection between cognitive and syntactic elements that operate within sentences. Suhor (1978) observes that:

> Studies of cognitive/syntactic matchups could effect significant changes in sentence-combining materials produced for the classroom. Exercises could be constructed around cognitive operations rather than grouped according to syntactic structures. Or, more likely, cognitive operations could be the main principle or organization, with the various syntactic settings subgrouped systematically under them. (10)

Consistent with the sentence-combining approach suggested by Suhor, our treatment did not organize activity according to syntactic structures. Such approaches have been historically constrained by the limited degree of interaction which they explicitly promote between sentence and text structures encoded by students. The generative approach developed by Christensen (1965, 1967, 1968) and adapted for sentence-combining activity by Strong (1973) is constrained from the onset by its emphasis on a limited number of structures--final, nonrestrictive elements. Indeed, only two studies generative rhetoric instruction (Bond, 1972 and Hazen, 1972) have found qualitative gains in student writing after 11-15 weeks of instruction. And Mellon (1979) was still discouraging structural approaches one decade after his pioneering study. He argued that "large syntactic-fluency increases must inevitably, sooner or later, boost quality scores," but he viewed "the concern for immediate over-all-quality improvement a turning away from serious writing research (37)."

The sentence-combining treatment that we developed and tested in our research imposed no such syntactic constraints on the instruction. That is to say, all structures recognized traditionally as elements of good usage were practiced in cued exercises. Based on the Pitkin model, propositions were syntactically combined in "x/y" fashion then grouped according to discourse functions that they support. Again, based on the Pitkin model, text structures were derived from the "x/y" relationship by modeling substage development in open sentence-combining exercises. The purpose of this approach was to improve the overall quality of students' writing by enhancing the interactions between syntactic and text-structure knowledge.

The next chapter reviews the research literature and the controversy in greater detail for the reader interested in such detail. Other readers may wish to skip to Chapter 3, which describes our instructional treatment and methodology, and return to Chapter 2 at a later time.

CHAPTER 2

RELATED LITERATURE

Sentence Combining

When Hunt (1965 a, b) began to study developmental differences based on deep-to-surface transformations, a construct he identified as "syntactic maturity," the modern sentence-combining era was born. To operationalize and quantify the variable, Hunt devised a new measure which he called the "minimal terminable unit" or "T-unit," and defined it as one main clause and any subordinate clause or nonclausal structure attached to or embedded in it. In turn, Hunt devised five measures, all ratios, three of which incorporated the T-unit: (1) mean words per sentence (w/s), (2) mean T-units per sentence (T/s), (3) mean words per T-unit (w/T), (4) mean clauses per T-unit (c/T), and (5) mean words per clause (w/c).

Using these five measures, Hunt analyzed the regular classroom composition of nine boys and nine girls within an average IQ range (90-110) in each of three grades--4, 8, and 12. In addition, Hunt analyzed 1000-word samples from 18 persons identified as "skilled adults"–each of whom had published in either Harper's Magazine or the Atlantic. Based on the data, Hunt concluded:

A.   As they mature, not only the children in grades 4-12 but also adults tend to write more words per clause.

B.   As they mature, children tend to write more clauses per T-unit, but the performance of skilled adults on this measure is not significantly greater than that of twelfth graders.

C.   Because w/T = w/c x c/T and because both measures (w/c and C/T) increase developmentally among schoolchildren, w/T displays parallel growth. The w/T measure increases among skilled adults because they write longer clauses.

D.   As they mature, children tend to write fewer T-units per sentence. The performance of skilled adults is most similar to children in the middle and upper grades.

E.   As they mature, children tend to write more words per sentence. Skilled adults reflect the same tendency. Because of the contradictory tendencies of w/T (which increases developmentally), words per sentence (the product of these contradictory measures) is not as good a measure as the others.

F.   Establishing the maturity of the average twelfth grader as the goal, the best measures of syntactic maturity are (in descending order): w/T, w/c, c/T, and w/s.

G.   Establishing the maturity of the average skilled adult as the goal, the best measures of syntactic maturity are identical to the preceding list, except that w/T and w/c are equally good.

Further analysis revealed to Hunt that the fourth graders' writing the greatest number of T-units per sentence results from their tendency to join clauses in run-on fashion. Among this group, these apparently less sophisticated writers combine clausal elements by using coordinating conjunctions like "and," not by subordination or by changing clausal to nonclausal elements. The tendency among fourth graders to combine thought in this way is three times greater than that of eighth graders and four times greater than that of twelfth graders. This data supports LaBrant's earlier conclusion that rejected sentence length as an index of maturity. Finally, Hunt observed that the tendency of the maturer writers to produce clauses and T-units of greater length was attributable to the types of transformation evident within these structures and not to the elaboration of simpler elements like auxiliaries.

Hunt's conclusions were supported by O'Donnell et al. (1967) who reported that "when fairly extensive samples of children's language are obtained, the mean length of T-units has special claim to consideration as a simple, objective, valid indicator of development in syntactic control." These investigators studied 30 children in each of grades K, 1, 2, 3, 5, 7, obtaining oral samples from all groups and written samples from students in grades 3, 5, and 7.

O'Donnell's data for T-unit length and clauses per T-unit parallels that of Hunt, revealing comparable trends among writing samples at the reported grade levels. (Although O'Donnell did not report mean clause length in his study, the data has been calculated from the other two measures.) Like Hunt, O'Donnell found that both T-unit and clause length in the students' writing increased with age. In addition to these measurements, O'Donnell also counted the number of transformations made by the students at the respective grade levels. His data supported Hunt's observation that the tendency of older students to write longer clauses and T-units was attributable to the number of transformations within these structures. In fact, O'Donnell remarked that parallels between the number of transformations and T-unit length at each grade level were "impressive."

Mellon (1969) acknowledged the developmental changes in free writing that occur as students mature, including the expansion of independent clauses, the elaboration of sentences, the increased use of subordinate elements, the employment of a wider range of sentence patterns, and more frequent and deeper embedding. He linked this continuous syntactic development--observed by Hunt and others--to cognitive development. Syntactic growth, he insisted, is not a substantive phenomenon but attributable to the students' (1) gaining greater experience in the world around them and (2) drawing more adult relations between their environment and themselves.

Mellon made a distinction between this growth–which he called syntactic maturity--and the observable range of sentence types employed by writers--which he called syntactic fluency. Mellon assumed that syntactic maturity occurs normally, without pedagogical intervention. But this normal growth, he asserted, need not be looked upon as optimal growth, "as the maximum permitted by some presumably fixed schedule of natural growth." He assumed that syntactic fluency could be enhanced by special treatment and proceeded to study whether grammar practice could enhance its growth.

To operationalize his dependent variable, Mellon identified twelve factors of syntactic fluency derived from pretest writing samples of his subjects collected in September. According to Mellon's (1969) analysis of the free writing of high-, average-, and low-ability seventh graders, the increased number or use of the following variables stipulatively defined the growth of syntactic fluency which the experimental treatment was designed to enhance:

1. Mean T-unit length.
2. Subordination-coordination ratio.
3. Nominal clauses per 100 T-units.
4. Nominal phrase per 100 T-units.
5. Relative clauses per 100 T-units.
6. Relative phrase per 100 T-units.
7. Relative words per 100 T-units.
8. Embedded kernel sentences per 100 T-units.
9. Cluster frequency.
10. Mean cluster size.
11. Embedded frequency.
12. Mean maximum depth level. (48-49)

The sentence-combining problems devised by Mellon were intended to connect the subjects' study of transformational grammar with the "pseudo-production of a range of sentences more mature in structure than typical of [their] writing at the time." The format of this activity was "cued," i.e. separate sentences could be transformed and combined only according to transformation-specific keys included within the problem format.

A problem like the following would be presented to the students at approximately the seventh month of treatment. Before attempting to solve this or any problem in the study, the students would have studied both the related transformations and the format details, the latter of which was described by Mellon as "purely mechanical and readily learned." The write-out or solution has been provided for this discussion.

PROBLEM

The children clearly must have wondered SOMETHING.
 The bombing had orphaned the children.
 SOMETHING was humanly possible somehow. (T: wh)
  Their conquerors pretended SOMETHING. (T: infin-
  T: exp)
   Chewing gum and smiles might compensate for
   the losses. (T: fact)
    The losses were heartbreaking.
    They had so recently sustained the losses.

WRITE OUT

The children who the bombing had orphaned clearly must have
wondered how it was humanly possible for their conquerors to
pretend that chewing gum and smiles might compensate for the
heart-breaking losses which they had so recently sustained.

Mellon first analyzed his pretest-posttest data to determine whether
growth had occurred in the experimental and control groups when
examined separately.   He found that the experimental group had
experienced significant growth at a low rate, well below the magnitude
to attain statistical significance.   In the second step of his analysis,
Mellon determined that the growth experienced by the experimentals
was significantly greater than that of the controls.

Although Mellon had provided strong evidence to suggest that a
systematic program of sentence combining will increase the rate at
which the sentence structure of a student's writing becomes more highly
elaborated, he was reluctant to conclude that growth in syntactic fluency
would necessarily lead to growth in either cognition or writing ability.
Indeed, his description of the new transformational, syntactic treatment

was accompanied by the disclaimer the "[Sentence combining] is <u>not</u> a program of composition or rhetoric, and it would neither replace or supplant such programs nor take over the subject matter for which they are responsible."

O'Hare (1973) thought otherwise. In a replication of Mellon's experiment, O'Hare hypothesized not only that the experimental group would score significantly higher on factors of syntactic maturity (O'Hare preferred "maturity" to Mellon's "fluency") but also that the experimental group would write compositions judged by eight experienced English teachers as significantly superior in overall quality to the compositions written by the control group.

Along with the addition of this important hypothesis, O'Hare modified the cuing system of the sentence-combining problems. O'Hare version of the previous problem written by Mellon was:

PROBLEM

The children clearly must have wondered SOMETHING.
The bombings had orphaned the children. (WHOM)
SOMETHING was humanly possible somehow. (WHY)
Their conquerors pretended SOMETHING. (IT-FOR-TO)
Chewing gum and smiles might compensate for their losses.
(THAT)
The loss was <u>heartbreaking</u>.
They had so recently sustained the losses. (WHICH)

The cuing modification allowed the student to solve the problem without previous instruction in grammar related to the cue itself. In addition, O'Hare found the series of indentations unnecessary and eliminated them. He did, however, retain in his format the capitalized word "SOMETHING", which signaled an open nominal position and which, in O'Hare's judgment, the students found helpful.

O'Hare reduced the number of dependent variables in his study from (Mellon's) twelve to six. The factors of syntactic maturity identified by O'Hare included: (1) Words per T-unit, (2) Clauses per T-unit, (3) Words per clause, (4) Noun clauses per 100 T-unit, (5) Adverb clauses per 100 T-units, and (6) Adjective clauses per 100 T-units. The single qualitative judgment of the compositions in O'Hare's study was based on five variables: (1) Ideas, (2) Organization, (3) Style, (4) Vocabulary, and (5) Sentence structure.

O'Hare's posttest data revealed that the experimentals had written significantly more and longer clauses than had the control group. Compared to Hunt's normative data, the level of maturity of the experimental's compositions exceeded that typical of eighth graders and, in many respects, was similar to that of twelfth graders. Additionally, the forced-choice holistic judgment of thirty pairs of experimental and control compositions resulted in the judges' selection of a significantly greater number of experimental compositions as superior.

Since the early experiments of Mellon and O'Hare, sentence-combining activity has consistently enhanced measures of syntactic maturity or fluency. A minority of studies (Gree, 1972; Ney, 1976; Waterfall, 1977) produced negative findings relative to syntactic maturity or fluency. Hillocks (1986) reported that about 60 percent of the studies report gains in fluency at $p<.05$ or better, and an additional 30 percent report varying levels of improvement. Based on her analysis of data from 427 students in grades 7-12, Rice (1983) found that sentence-combining activity produces a mean gain of 15 percentile points over a 10-week period on measures of syntactic maturity.

Researchers, however, have used varied procedures for testing, analysis, and measurement which can make difficult the comparison and interpretation of results. The size of the experimental population varies widely among studies, from ten (Vitale et al., 1971), 14 (Maimon and Nodine, 1979), and 18 (Hilfman, 1970) to 335 (Hunt and O'Donnell, 1970) and 247 (Mellon, 1969). The testing material is typically a sample of either free or controlled-content writing, the latter of which resembles Hunt's "Aluminum" passage. Differences in student performance related to each measure have been reported and supported, with samples of free writing yielding consistently higher scores. In addition, free-writing procedures have been criticized for lack of standardization; controlled samples, for insensitivity to varying densities of content at different age levels.

The length of the writing sample reveals the arbitrary tendencies of sentence-combining researchers. Miller and Ney (1967), Perron (1974), and Straw (1978) collected 300-word samples from fourth graders, while Stewart (1978) collected samples of the sample length from college freshman. In his attempt to collect approximately 1000 words from each of his seventh graders, Mellon (1969) used the first ten T-units from each of nine different samples. In his replication of Mellon's study, O'Hare (1973) collected the first ten 10 units from only five samples. Still later, Combs (1975) and Pederson (1977) collected the first 15 T-units of only two samples at the same grade level.

Studies have indicated that mode of discourse--narration, description, exposition, and argumentation--influences syntactic performance in writing (Mellon, 1969; San Jose, 1972, 1976; Crowhurst, 1977; Crowhurst and Piche, 1979). Some sentence-combining researchers (Perron, 1974; O'Hare, 1973; Sullivan, 1977; Callaghan, 1977) have used all four modes. Others (Green, 1972; Ofsa, 1974; Combs, 1975; Pedersen, 1977; Mulder et al., 1978) have used two modes. In the only sentence-combining finding related to the differential effect of discourse modes, Green (1972) concluded that clause length was increased in narration but not in exposition.

Definitive procedures for unit segmentation simply do not exist. Hunt's criteria have apparently been followed by most subsequent researchers--with the notable exception of Mellon (1969). Studies, however, are characteristically vague on the topic of T-unit segmentation, simply making reference to previous studies. Brereton (1979) not only found procedural differences among different affected T-unit counts.

Most recently, Strong (1986) suggested that the two most significant and persistent inconsistencies in much of the SC research are the duration of treatment and the treatment conditions themselves. Of the former inconsistency, Kerek et al. (1980) observe that determining the optimal duration of treatment is made difficult by research variables like: span of treatment, duration of students' involvement in SC activity, and the frequency and intensity of this involvement. Strong notes:

> The two key variables--the type of SC and the process for teaching it--often get surprisingly little attention. An inevitable consequence is conflicting results; but equally important, one cannot discern the types of materials and teaching approaches most likely to produce payoff. (7)

In his meta-analysis of experimental composition treatments, Hillocks (1984) concluded that "research shows sentence combining, on the average, to be more than twice as effective as free writing as a means of enhancing the quality of student writing." However, in some case studies (Mellon, 1969; Perron, 1974; Sullivan, 1977; Callaghan, 1977; Stewart, 1978), the experimental students did not achieve superiority in overall writing quality.

Some of the research ambiguity may be explained in terms of duration of treatment. Studies in which sentence-combining activity was conducted between ten and twelve hours over several weeks of instruction have found no significant difference in measures of overall writing quality between experimental and control subjects. According to Jones (1980), maximum potential writing growth will not likely occur among college freshmen prior to 20 hours of sentence-combining activity over a 10-week period.

It is likely that most of the inconsistency among findings concerning sentence combining's effect on overall writing quality is attributable to the varied instructional procedures of the researchers. The early investigations of both Mellon (1969) and O'Hare (1973) used cued exercises structured exclusively around single-sentence, syntactic problems devoid of context. In an approach which he dubbed "decomposition-recomposition," Ney (1976) decomposed--i.e. reduced to kernel and attached or embedded propositions--sentences derived from classic prose read by his student, then cued the recomposition of the propositions in single-sentence exercises. Ney believed that this manner of establishing context provided the most appropriate "ideational setting for the exercise."

Callaghan (1977) and Sullivan (1977) introduced a method of paragraph combining which they called "reconstitution ." In these exercises, students weighed practiced syntactic options in the context of "the whole piece" of discourse. Stewart (1978) presented uncued or "open" sentence-combining problems to his college freshmen, modeling the activity after Christensen's generative rhetoric which emphasizes the expansion of sentences by the addition of different types of "free" modifiers. Although measures of syntactic maturity were significantly enhanced among Stewart's experimental subjects, similar gains were not achieved in measures of overall writing quality. Like Stewart, Faigley (1979) modeled his treatment for college freshmen after Christensen's generative rhetoric, but unlike Stewart, Faigley demonstrated significant growth in measures of both syntactic maturity and overall writing quality. However, in a stepwise regression analysis of his six syntactic variables as predictors of holistic ratings, Faigley discovered that in combination the six variables could explain only 22 percent of the variance in holistic scores.

Because it is uncued, the open format devised by Strong (1973) can generate a range of grammatically appropriate responses to sentence-combining problems. Its objective is the exploration of stylistic options. In their study of 290 Miami University (Oxford, Ohio) freshmen, Daiker et al. presented twelve model exercises and 27 whole-discourse exercises, all of which were open in design and "deliberately and unabashedly rhetorical in character." Intensive practice at the sentence (model) level of combining was integrated within a rhetorical (whole-discourse) context. The Miami study showed significant gains in the experimental groups not only on measures of syntactic fluency but also on forced-choice, holistic, and analysis measures of overall writing quality. However, in the Miami study, covariance analysis indicated that the experimental students significantly outperformed the conventionally trained students in five of six analytic categories: (1) ideas, (2) supporting details, (3) voice, (4) sentence structure, and (5) diction/usage. The experimental difference was not large enough in the category of organization/coherence to be statistically significant.

The proposed treatment is based on the assumption of Pitkin (1977), who represents coherent discourse as the product of the combination of ideas for some functional purpose. Pitkin argues that this cognitive process is a binary operation which links two base-level propositions hierarchically to satisfy some discourse strategy. Such assumptions are closely aligned to the tenets of transformational grammar and lend themselves naturally to sentence-combining activity.

Although Pitkin pays much attention to the syntactic forms that link propositions and give discourse its most rudimentary structure, the organizational principle of his pedagogical model of discourse focuses on specific cognitive operations, with various syntactic settings subgrouped systematically under them. And although Pitkin does not suggest sentence-combining activity as an effective method for implementing his ideas, Suhor (1978) notes the appropriateness of the instructional strategy:

> (C)ognitive/syntactic matchups could effect significant change in sentence-combining materials for classroom use...(For example), students might be given sentence-combining exercises to promote greater variety and elasticity in the expression of conditionality, beginning with a more commonplace syntactic setting (e.g., and adverb clause with the lexical clue

"if") and moving on the structures less commonly used for hosting conditionality (e.g., absolute phrases like "weather permitting,..."). (10)

Sentence-combining approaches to writing instruction, as Rose (1983) notes, were in evidence in turn-of-the-century texts. Since that time, many methodological variations have evolved. However, none have orchestrated the "cognitive/syntactic matchups" devised by Pitkin, in a general pedagogical model, and advocated by Suhor, as did we in our study.

CHAPTER 3

VARIABLES AND METHODOLOGY

Overview

Our research investigated the influence of discourse-function sentence combining on the expository writing of ninth graders. The discourse-function sentence-combining activities have both cued and open response formats. The treatment was divided into eight units, each of which was organized around discourse strategies adapted from Pitkin (1977).

In each of the eight instructional units, all subjects were initially required to semantically map a specific chapter of their ninth-grade biology text and define new vocabulary. This activity represented an attempt to control knowledge difference between the experimental and control subjects. Subjects were randomly assigned to the experimental or control groups.

In each of the eight instructional units, the experimental subjects completed one cued then one open sentence-combining activity following the mapping exercises. At the same time, the control subjects completed traditional grammar and usage exercises from Warriner's English Grammar and Composition, Third Course, 1977.

At the conclusion of each of the eight units, all subjects completed an in-class expository writing assignment whose topic was related to the biology chapter mapped at the beginning of the unit. The writing assignment submitted at the conclusion of the final (eighth) instructional unit was the posttest. Prior to the experiment, an expository theme was completed by all subjects as one component of the placement battery, administered to all eighth-grade applicants to the school in the late spring, three months prior to the beginning of the treatment. This late-spring assessment of the subjects' writing was used as the pretest.

The two dependent variables investigated in our study were writing quality and syntactic maturity. The writing quality of the pretest expository writing task, as well as the eight expository writing task, as well as the eight expository writing task administered during the experimental period, were measured in two ways. First, the overall quality of the subjects' performance was judged by three experienced high-school English teachers using a 4-point holistic instrument. In addition, writing quality was assessed by the same team of teachers with an analytic instrument whose criteria are: organization, main ideas, details, cohesion, sentence structure, and usage. The syntactic maturity of all writing tasks was measured by the calculation of words per t-unit, clauses per t-unit, and words per clause in the manner prescribed by Hunt (1965).

One expository written task was administrated at the conclusion of each of the eight instructional weeks to all subjects. Each of the eight tasks required the subjects to discuss the biology content which they had mapped and discussed at the beginning of the week. The subjects were allowed to refer to their maps while they were writing. In addition, each task requires the subjects to structure the essay in a manner consistent with a specific discourse function. For example, during the fourth week, all subjects initially mapped chapter 12 of their biology text. The chapter discussed "Blood." At the conclusion of the week, all subjects were instructed to use pertinent content from the chapter to structure a cause-and-effect response to the following stimulus: "Explain why an organism would die within minutes if it's heart stopped beating." All expository writing tasks were completed within the 42-minute class, and all were at least ten sentences in length.

The study was conducted in a suburban regional technical high school located in the northeastern region of the United States. The center for Labor Market Studies at Northeastern University (1993) reported that the five towns comprising the region have an aggregate population of 119,000. The major occupations of the 65, 494 employed regional residents include professional and related service (24%), manufacturing (22%), and retails (17%). The mean household income within the region is $56,819. Ninety-five percent of the regional population are white; one percent is black; one percent Hispanic; and two percent Asian and Pacific Islanders. Based on (1) their performance on the "Reading Comprehension" subtest of the Stanford Diagnostic Reading Test, (2) their performance an expository writing sample which is holistically scored by members of the school's English department, and (3) current special Needs (chapter 766) stipulations, students are grouped homogeneously within mainstream or special Needs English programs at the school. Mainstreamed English students are homogeneously grouped in five levels. Level one is the honors program; and level two is the college-prep program; levels three and four are the general literature and language program; and levels, students with individual educational plans specifying segregated instructional environments receive English instruction from the proposed experiment were the mainstreamed level-4 students. Based on the preceding placement criteria, these students were judged to be within an average to low-average range of verbal ability.

Subjects

Approximately 120 ninth-grade students, 80 males and 40 females, participated in the study. These students, who comprised the entire 4-level population of ninth-grade English students at the school, were judged to be of average to low-average verbal ability based on their performance on (1) the "Reading Comprehension" subtest of the Stanford Diagnostic Reading Test (SDRT). 1985, Blue Level, form G and (2) the Shawsheen Writing Test, Form B (See Appendix A.)

To establish the reliability of the SDRT subtest, the Psychological Corporation (1998), its publisher, reports a KR-20 reliability coefficient of .92 and a standard error of measurement of 2.9. Consistent with the advice of the publisher, the school determined the content curricular validity of the instrument based on a comparison of the subtest's content and the content constituted a representative sample of skills and knowledge addressed in the curriculum. The same panel of experienced teachers participated in the design of the Shawsheen Writing Test (SWT) and unanimously agreed that the instrument was a valid means of eliciting an essay that contrasts two ideas or views.   On the SWT, students must write an essay about effective and ineffective teachers and their teaching styles.

The 4-level subjects participate in this study typically score between 2 and 3 on a 4-point holistic assessment of the SWT pretest (comparison/contrast) writing task.   Their mean SDRT "Reading Comprehension" grade equivalence score is 7.2 which suggests that the 4-level, ninth-grade population of the school is developmentally similar to seventh graders.   These students were selected precisely for this reason; namely, for their potential readiness to demonstrate considerable growth on measures of syntactic maturity.

The preceding readiness hypothesis is based on investigations of students' syntactic maturity at five grade levels.   According to the parallel investigations of Hunt (1965) and later O'Donnell (1967), the mean length of T-unit is a valid and special indicator of development in syntactic control.   In these studies, seventh graders demonstrated uniquely large gains.   Although mean T-unit length increased by only 2.1 words between grades 3 and 7, the measure increased by nearly 1.7 words between grades 7 and 8.   The investigators also found that, to a lesser but considerable extent, two other measures, the mean number of clauses per T-unit and mean words per clause, increased during this developmental period.

Although the preceding hypothesis suggests that the 4-level ninth graders who participated in the experiment can be compared to younger students, it acknowledges that ninth graders who are two years below grade level on standardized measures of performance or intelligence are not necessarily similar to seventh graders who score at grade level on the same measures.

Within the academic environment of the technical high school, all students were randomly assigned by computer to English section within each of five ability levels.   Based on the admission data, six 4-level English sections (n=120) were formed.   These sections were similar in terms of the students' writing and reading ability as measured by the placement-battery instruments.   The actual statistical equivalence was checked using the SDRT and Shawsheen Writing Test premeasures that are available on students.

Since all 4-level students were assigned identical courses in other academic disciplines, confounding variables related to different academic experiences were minimized in this school.   In addition, no students participating in the experiment received direct instructions in either narrative reading or expository writing by their English teachers proceeding the experimental period.

Design and Treatment

For the holistic and analytic ratings of writing effectiveness, as well as for the three factors of syntactic maturity, a pretest-posttest control group design was used. This design takes the form:

$$R \; O_1 \; X_e \; O_2$$
$$R \; O_3 \; X_c \; O_4$$

Both the pretest and posttest are expository writing tasks whose validity was established in the manner described in the Instrumentation section of this chapter. Both writing tasks elicited similar (comparison/contrast) responses from the students. The pretest was administered to all eighth-grade applicants to the school as the composition component of the school's battery of placement tests between May and August preceding their admission. The post-test was the last of eight expository writing tasks assigned to all experimental and control students during the experimental period. The treatment consisted of eight weeks of sentence-combining instruction which occurred January to June, during the school's third and fourth marking periods. The 8-week treatment period extended through these 18 calendar weeks because students attend academic classes only during alternate weeks at the technical high school. Table 3.1 identifies the 8-week schedule of biology topics, discourse functions, and writing tasks. The topics were taken from eight chapters of the biology text used by 4-level ninth graders who participated in the experiment. The discourse functions are based on Pitkin's discourse strategies. The writing tasks, discussed further in the Instrumentation section of the chapter, required the students to apply both biology and discourse-function knowledge.

Campbell and Stanley (1963) observe that the pretest-posttest control group design controls neatly for most rival hypotheses, but they issue specific warnings. Among those warnings, the unanticipated occurrence of differential intrasession history is discussed at some length. In the attempt to control confounding variables associated with intrasession history and other factors, instructional units for both the

Table 3.1. An 8-Week Schedule of Biology Topics, Discourse Functions, and
Expository Writing Tasks

Week	Biology Topic	Discourse Function	Writing Task
1	Nutrition	Series Coordination	Identify and discuss the important features of a balanced diet.
2	Digestive System	Assertion-Inclusion	Describe what happens to food from the time it enters the mouth until it leaves the large intestine.
3	Circulatory System	Assertion-Significance	Trace the path of a drop of blood from the toe cell, through the circulatory system, then back to the toe cell.
4	Blood	Cause and Effect	Explain why an organism would die within minutes if its heart stopped beating.
5	Respiratory, Urinary Systems	Manner-, Evaluation-, Time-, and Location-Assertion	Describe how waste materials are removed from the blood.
6	Skeletal, Muscular Systems	Assertion-Intensification Assertion-Regression	Describe how your life would change if you suddenly did not have a skeleton.
7	Nervous, Endocrine Systems	Assertion-Comparison	The nervous system is commonly compared to a telephone system whose switchboard is the brain. Describe how messages travel through this system.
8	Animal Reproduction	Assertion-Contrast	Contrast the male and female reproductive systems.

experimental and control group began with the semantic mapping exercises which reviewed the biology content on which the expository writing tasks were based. The mapping activity introduced main ideas and details which were pertinent to the writing task but which might have been inadvertently or intentionally omitted by the content teachers.

Since biology is taught by four teachers at the school and since these teachers do not follow the same sequence of topics during the academic year, the mapping exercises additionally ensured that all subjects had at least one exposure to the content. However, since the experiment was conducted during the third and fourth terms, and since the majority of the students covered the topics concurrently or just prior to that time, the mapping exercises served as a review and as a control for instructional recency. Also, the mapping activities ensured that all students were prepared to write in similar fashion and that observed differences in writing were not primarily due to the treatment and variables examined in this study. In addition to the pretest-posttest comparison, all interim writing tasks were assessed with the same instructions to measure any treatment-by-discourse-function interactions that might have occurred.

Following the mapping exercise, each of the eight lessons provided practice in both cued and open sentence-combining activity. In each lesson, both the cued and open exercises modeled syntactic and paragraphing strategies for achieving a specific discourse function. The cued activity required the students to combine signaled content contained in series of sentences in order to rewrite that content in one syntactically more complex sentence. Each cued activity presented approximately ten such rewriting tasks to the students.

Open sentence-combining is an instructional technique that involves the fading of the cues around which the preceding exercises were structured. Instead of eliciting specific responses from specific cues, the open exercises introduce stimulus generalization. None of the content in the open passages is underlined, and none appeared within parentheses. In the open exercises, a student is encouraged to make any one of a set of acceptable responses based on the syntactic options which were practiced in the cued exercises. Instead of responding by writing a new sentence, the students must produce new paragraphs. The open exercises progressively expand the length of the rewriting task.

Each of the eight open exercises presented three rewriting tasks which were one, two, and three paragraphs in length respectively. Examples of the open sentence-combining exercises are included in the Appendix.

Directions to the students in each of the open exercises possessed specific features. Students were initially invited to study the passage for the purpose of rewriting them in a better way. Next, the students were advised to focus on the topic statements and combine them using a syntactic option appropriate to the discourse function. Then, the students were advised to rewrite the rest of the passage to create a better, more mature style. Finally, the directions stipulated that students may change the order of words and omit redundant or unnecessary words. Students were warned, however, against deleting information.

The open material provided for the students also possessed specific features. In each lesson, the open exercises consisted of three passages which were one, two, and three paragraphs in length respectively. Like the content of the cued exercised, the content of each open passage pertained to a topic discussed in a specified chapter of the students' biology text. In each unit, the three open passages discussed three different topics. Each passage was titled. The topic statements in each passage appeared in upper-case letters to make them immediately evident to the students. Like the cued exercises, each open passage was followed by blank lines on which the students were instructed to write their responses.

The teachers who participated in the piloting of the experimental materials unanimously agreed that the open exercises were instructionally worthwhile. They observed that the passages not only gradually expanded the context of discourse while fading the cues, but also provided good models of cohesive writing after the completion of the activity. The same teachers warned, however, that the open exercises should not be duplicated or modified as tests. The teachers explained that, although students could respond immediately to the cued exercises, the open activity presented a significantly greater challenge to some. They added that testing students' ability to complete the open exercises would likely frustrate the 4-level ninth graders, particularly during the beginning of the treatment period. The teachers strongly suggested that the absence of testing would provide more time both to discuss the process of creating cohesive discourse and to examine the products. Based on these recommendations, the open sentence-combining exercises were used only as instructional activities in this study.

Each lesson concluded with an expository writing activity which required the students to write a composition of at least ten sentences in length in response to a stimulus associated with the biology topic. Unlike the sentence-combining exercises, neither cues nor sentence content was provided. Students used only their semantic maps as a reference during this activity, which were completed during a 42-minute class period. Table 3.2 identified the experimental subjects' activities during a regular, 9-meeting academic week. All instruction was completed by the conclusion of he sixth meeting each week. During the remaining three meetings, the mapping, sentence-combining, and writing tests were administered.

Table 3.2. Weekly Schedule of Experimental-Group Classes

Class	Activity
1	Survey biology-text chapter. Fill-out map. Assign definition homework.
2	Complete map if necessary. Begin cued sentence-combining exercises.
3	Check definition homework. Discuss logic of subtopic sequence, topic-subtopic relationships, and subtopic-detail relationships.
4	Complete cued sentence-combining exercises. Begin open sentence-combining exercises.
5	Continue open sentence-combining exercises.
6	Complete open sentence-combining exercises. Practice cued sentence-combining test (time permitting.)
7	Take map test.
8	Take cued sentence-combining test.
9	Take expository writing test.

During the third and fourth marking periods of the 1992-1993 academic year, four members of the English Department at the regional technical high school piloted the experimental program. During that periods, weekly meetings were held with these staff to discuss the treatment. As a result, some modifications were made in the pilot materials and scheduling, and those staff became acquainted and comfortable with the materials and instructional schedule. Three of the staff were, at the time, assigned 4-level ninth-grade English classes, and they subsequently participated in the experiment.

At the end of each week, two tests were administered to measure the students' knowledge of (1) the organization of the biology content as presented in their text and (2) the discourse strategy.   The knowledge-of –organization measure required the students to fill-in a blank map, identical in design and content to the map completed earlier in the week (See Appendix B).   The knowledge-of-discourse measure required the students to complete cued sentence combining exercises which is, again, a duplication of the class activity (See Appendix C). Both the map and cued sentence-combining tests were scored by percent correct of total responses. Students' scores were recorded each week and across the treatment period to assess the correlation of each (map and sentence-combining) measure with each other and to the dependent variables.   Finally, the expository writing assignment (See Appendix D) was produced during one 42-minute class session and was assessed by trained raters to measure the holistic, analytic , and syntactic variable. As Table 3.3 outlines, the control students began each week with identical mapping exercises and were subsequently engaged in traditional syntax activity.

Table 3.3. Weekly Schedule of Control-Group Classes

Class	Activity
1	Survey biology-text chapter. Fill-out map. Assign definition homework.
2	Complete map if necessary. Discuss grammar topic (1)..
3	Check definition homework. Discuss logic of subtopic sequence, topic-subtopic relationships, and subtopic-detail relationships.
4	Discuss grammar topic (2).
5	Discuss grammar topic (3).
6	Discuss grammar topic (4).
7	Take map test.
8	Take grammar test.
9	Take expository writing test.

Table 3.4 identifies the syntax topics which were taught to the control subjects during the experimental period.   Appendix Table E identifies the specific in-class exercises, homework assignments, and syntax-knowledge tests which comprised the control-group's activities

during the experimental period. These activities were taken from Warriner's English Grammar and Composition, Third Course (1977), a text currently used in the ninth-grade curriculum at the school. At the end of the week, the control students were administered mapping tests and expository writing exercises identical to those assigned to the experimental students. In addition to these measures, the control students were administered the traditional syntax-knowledge test identified in the appendix table.

Table 3.4. An 8-Week Schedule of Control-Group Syntax Topics

Week	Topics
1	Common and proper nouns; capitalization; personal, reflexive, relative, interrogative, and demonstrative pronouns.
2	Case forms of personal pronouns, prepositions and objects.
3	Actions verbs, linking verbs, verb phrases.
4	Agreement of pronoun and antecedent, agreement of subject and verb.
5	The adjective, the adverb.
6	Verbals, verb phrases.
7	Appositives, punctuation of parenthetical expressions, punctuation of compound sentences.
8	Independent and subordinate clauses.

Instrumentation

According to Ausubel (1968), cognitive mapping is an activity that aids retention of specific content by clarifying and organizing an individual's schema prior to a learning task. Because most students studied the biology chapters used in this study at different times prior to the treatment period, the mapping exercises attempted to control for instructional recency. In addition, the exercise attempted to control for instructional differences resulting from the students' exposure to four or five different biology teachers.

For the purpose of this study, the mapping exercises presented both the control and experimental students with blank maps at the beginning of each of the eight instructional units. Each blank map consisted of a central circle in which the students identified the main topic of a specific chapter from their biology text. The central circle is surrounded by a series of other circles, whose number corresponded to the number of subtopics in the specified chapter. At the top of each of these circles, students identified one subtopic. For the purpose of comprehending the organizational logic of the chapter, the subtopics were identified in the same order as that in which they were discussed in the text. With in each circle, the students identified the important details related to the respective subtopics. Numbered, blank lines were provided within each circles to accommodate the writing of the details. The number of lines corresponded to the number of bold-face details which appeared under each subtopic in the specified chapter.

Students filled-in the map's topic , subtopic, and detail information during whole-class activity guided by the teacher. Thus, by the conclusion of each class' second meeting each week, all students possessed identical maps of the specified chapter. The students were then instructed to study the map for a test which was scheduled for the last meeting of each week. The test presented each student with a blank form identical to the map completed earlier in the week. Accompanying the map, the test also provided each student with an alphabetized list of all terms which must appear within the circles. The list did not identify or subgroup topics, subtopics, and details. The intent of the list was to reduce the recall burden for the students, allowing them to attend to the organizational logic of the chapter without compelling them to memorize lists of terms. The map tests were scored as simple percent of total responses correct. That data was recorded by unit and across the treatment period to correlate those scores to the students' expository writing performances.

Cued sentence combining is an individual component of a complex skill. For the purpose of this study, cued sentence combining is a task that required the student to respond to specific cues or signals in a series of sentences in order to create a new sentence that expressed an idea in the context of a specific discourse strategy (e.g. cause and effect). The combined product is usually but not necessarily longer and syntactically more complex. Examples of cued exercises are included in the Appendix.

Underlined and parenthetical cues were used in this study. The cues identified the content that was combined to form the new sentence. Underlined content was included verbatim in the new sentence. Parenthetical content that followed a sentence was included verbatim in the new sentence. Parenthetical content was inserted into the new sentence in a position that preceded underlined content for the same sentence. The students wrote their responses, the new sentences, in spaces provided after the series of cued sentences.

Eighty-five cued items were written for this study. Table 3.5 identifies (1) the syntactic structures that are cued in each of the items and (2) the distribution of those items among the eight lessons that comprise the treatment.

Table 3.5. Distribution of Cued Syntactic Structures by Discourse Function and Item.

Lesson Number and Discourse Function	Lesson Item											
	1	2	3	4	5	6	7	8	9	10	11	12
1 Series Coordination	A	A	B	A	C	C	C	D	C	C	E	E
2 Assertion-Inclusion	G	G	G	G	G	G	G	G	G	GF		
				C	D	F	F	F	F			
3 Assertion-Significnce	G	G	D	D	F	F	H	H	I	I		
4 Cause and Effect	F	J	F	F	F	C	F	F	D	F	I	
5 M,T,L,E-Assertion	E	E	E	E	E	F	F	D	F	D		
6 Assertion-Intensifictn	E	C	E	E	K	K						
Assertion-Regression							K	K	K	K	K	K
7 Assertion-Comparisn	C	F	C	F	L	G	D	A	A	C		
8 Assertion-Contrast	C	M	C	I	F	B	I	I	I	G		

Syntactic structure codes:

A=Correlative conjunctions
B=Coordinating conjunction
C=Prepositional phrase
D=Participial phrase
E=Adverb (single word)
F=Dependent clause
G=Appostive

H=Compound verb
I=Compound sentence
J=Infinitive phrase
K=Nonrestrictive phrase
L=Predicate noun (metaphor)
M=Adjective phrase

The syntactic structures that support each of the eight discourse functions duplicate those identified by Pitkin (1997). For the most part, the syntactic structures modeled by Pitkin for each of his discourse functions accommodated the writing of ten cued sentence-combining items. The number of items in lessons one and four exceeds ten due to the variety of expressions and structures modeled by Pitkin for these discourse functions. The number of items in lesson six exceeds ten because two closely related functions, Assertion-Comparison and

Assertion-Regression, were combined to form one lesson.

Table 3.6 indicates the distribution of the 13 syntactic structures throughout the eight lessons. As the table indicates, the treatment pays much attention to clausal and phrasal sentence elements which the ninth grader can use to structure syntactically maturer ideas. Additionally, the treatment focuses on words that join ideas (conjunctions) or provide cohesive transitions between and among them (adverbs).

Table 3.6. Cued sentence Combining: Distribution of Cued Syntactic Structures by DiscourseFunction.

Syntactic Structure	Discourse Function								
	1	2	3	4	5	6	7	8	T
Dependent clause	1	5	2	7	3	0	2	1	21
Appositive	0	10	2	0	0	0	1	0	13
Prepositional phrase	5	1	0	1	0	1	3	2	13
Adverb (single wrd)	1	0	0	0	5	3	0	0	9
Nonrestrictve phrase	0	0	0	0	0	8	0	0	8
Participial phrase	1	1	2	1	2	0	1	0	8
Compound sentence	0	0	2	1	0	0	0	4	7
Correlative conj	3	0	0	0	0	0	2	0	5
Coordinating conj	1	0	0	0	0	0	0	2	3
Compound verb	0	0	2	0	0	0	0	0	2
Infinitive	0	0	0	1	0	0	0	0	1
Predicate noun	0	0	0	0	0	0	1	0	1
Adjective phrase	0	0	0	0	0	0	0	1	1
Total	12	17	10	11	10	12	10	10	92

Functions

1=Series Coordination	5=M-, E-, T-, L-Assertion
2=Assertion-Inclusion	6=Assertion-Intensification, -Regression
3=Assertion-Significance	7=Assertion-Comparison
4=Cause and Effect	8=Assertion-Contrast

Two panels of experienced secondary teachers established the content validity of the cued exercises. The team of four experienced English teachers, who piloted the materials at the school, reviewed the cued exercises at the conclusion of each lesson to determine the appropriateness of the syntactic structures to the respective discourse functions. These individuals unanimously approved the 85 items which comprise the cued activities. In addition, three members of the Science Department reviewed the cued materials to judge whether or not the lessons presented the biology content accurately. These individuals found no factual errors in the lessons.

As the Table 3.2 indicates, the experimental group worked with the cued sentence-combining instrument twice during each of the eight instructional weeks. From the second through the fourth classes, the student solved the cued problem in class with teacher guidance. During this activity both the underlined and parenthetical cues were present. However when the cued instrument was administered during the eighth class as a measure of syntactic ability, the underlined cues were deleted from the instrument. All parenthetical information remained.

The deletion results from the consensus of the teachers who piloted the instrument. Those teachers observed that students attended less to sentences and their meaning and more to only the underlined cues when those cues were present on the test instrument. The teachers reported that most students freely admitted to this short-cut approach during discussion of test-taking strategies.

After the underlined cues were deleted, students reported that they were compelled to read the sentence, and attend to both meaning and structure in order to formulate the new sentence. Although a statistical comparison of scores under both test conditions was not made, the teachers reported that the students' performance did not decline with the cue deletion. Since a discourse-function treatment must assume that students are attending to the discourse, and since the deletion of the underlined cues required the students to focus on the discourse without apparently changing the level of their test performance, the underlined cues were deleted in all cued test instruments.

The cued tests were scored by simple percent of total responses correct. For example, each item in a 10-item test was worth ten points. If, in this 10-item test, five cues must be combined to write the new sentence, each cue was worth two points. Students' scores were recorded each week and across the treatment period to assess their correlation to the dependent variables.

In the present study, each of the eight instructional units concluded with one expository writing exercise which, like the other instruments and materials, are modeled in the Appendix. The expository writing exercises eliminated all syntactic cues. Unlike cued and open sentence-combining activity, expository writing exercises provided neither prewritten sentences nor paragraphs. Since students can infer appropriate syntactic links between prewritten, related, and juxtaposed sentences, the elimination of these ideas constituted the elimination of cues.

Each exercise assigns a specific writing task related to a specific biology topic. A panel of experienced, secondary biology teachers established the content validity of each biology topic. Besides the task, only brief directions were included in the activity. Those directions advised the students to think about the content of the specified biology chapter. The students were further advised that they could refer to their cognitive maps of the biology chapter as memory aids. Finally, the directions stipulated ten (10) sentences, organized as one or more paragraphs, as the minimum length of response. The expository writing tasks were assessed by raters using both the syntactic and analytic instruments described in the Scoring section of this chapter. The data was analyzed in the manner described in the Analysis section of this chapter.

Schedule of Data Collection

During the experimental period, subjects attended academic classes on the week-about schedule that is typical of Massachusetts technical-school programming. In this format, students attended academic and shop classes during alternative weeks. Thus, an 8-week period occurred within 16 calendar weeks.

One expository writing task was composed by all experimental and control students on the Friday that concluded each of the eight academic weeks in the treatment period. Eight expository writing tasks were composed by both groups during the 8-week treatment period. Each of the eight tasks was assessed during the shop week subsequent to the academic week in which they were written.

Instrument Scoring

The assessment of each expository writing task occurred in three phases. The first phase began on Friday of the academic week and ended on Monday of the shop week. During that 4-day period, the syntactic variables were scored by six English teachers. For the purpose of scoring the syntactic measures, each of the six teachers was assigned one of the six classes participating in the experiment. Each teacher scored the syntactic measures of the writing tasks composed by the students assigned to him or her. All of these teachers possess Master Degrees in English, and they average 17 years of teaching experience.

Figure 3.7 illustrates the form that was used to score the syntactic variables. Hunt (1965 a, b) and O'Donnell (1967) established the predictive validity of five measures of syntactic maturity. Hunt observed that, establishing the maturity of the average twelfth graders as the goal, the three best developmental measures of syntactic maturity are: T-unit length, clauses per T-unit, and clause length. As the preceding chapter discussed, the present study will use these three measures to assess the treatment's effect on Hunt and O'Donnell's construct.

Table 3.7. Instrument for Quantifying Syntactic Variables

Student		Section		Assignment	
	Words	Clauses		Words	Clauses
T-Unit 1			T-Unit 11		
T-Unit 2			T-Unit 12		
T-Unit 3			T-Unit 13		
T-Unit 4			T-Unit 14		
T-Unit 5			T-Unit 15		
T-Unit 6			T-Unit 16		
T-Unit 7			T-Unit 17		
T-Unit 8			T-Unit 18		
T-Unit 9			T-Unit 19		
T-Unit 10			T-Unit 20		
Total Words (A)					
Total Clauses (B)					
Total T-Units (C)					
Mean Words Per Clause (A/B)					
Mean Clauses Per T-Unit (B/C)					
Mean Words Per T-Unit (A/C)					

In this study, the rules for segmenting and counting T-units are those developed by Hunt (1965) and adopted by others (O'Donnell et al., 1967; O'Hare, 1973; Combs, 1975; Pedersen, 1977; Kerek et al., 1980). A T-unit is defined as one main clause and any subordinate clause or phrase appended to it. A subordinate clause, group of words contain a subject and a verb, does not express a complete thought and, therefore, cannot stand alone. Segmenting is a procedure which identifies T-units and any subordinate clauses appended to them. In the segmenting, double slashes are used to mark the beginning and end of each T-unit, and single slashes are used to mark each subordinate clause. The following passage illustrated this style of segmenting:

> //Certain white blood cells have the job of making special chemicals called antibodies. //Antibodies are chemicals /that help destroy a bacterium or virus. //Antibodies keep us healthy by getting rid of antigens /that enter our bodies. //Antigens are foreign substances //that are usually proteins /which invade the body and cause diseases.//

Using the Table-3.7 instrument, the preceding passage would be analyzed in the manner illustrated by Table 3.8.

Two other rules necessarily accompany this general style of analysis. Theses two rules concern what constitutes a word and how to deal with certain punctuation. First, a "word" is defined as a group of letters between blank spaces. This definition is extended to include dates (October 26), cities and states (New York), and compound proper nouns (Boston Garden). Hyphenated compounds (peace-loving) and contractions (we're, you'd), however, are counted as two words. Further, any fragment mispunctuated as a sentence counted within the T-unit it properly joins. The attention paid to clauses in direct and indirect quotations by other investigators was not a concern in this study because students did not quote or cite excerpt of the biology text in the content of the expository writing tasks.

The second assessment phase occurred between Tuesday and Thursday of the shop week. The third assessment phase occurred between the ensuing Friday and Sunday. During each of these phases, each expository writing task was assessed analytically and holistically by one of three raters. The design allowed inter-intrarater possess Masters Degrees in English, and they average 15 years of teaching experience.

Table 3.8. An Example Syntactic Analysis.

Student 14		Section 3	Assignment 2		
	Words	Clauses		Words	Clauses
T-Unit 1	*13*	*1*	T-Unit 11	*15*	*2*
T-Unit 2	*10*	*2*	T-Unit 12		
T-Unit 3	*13*	*2*	T-Unit 13		
T-Unit 4	*15*	*3*	T-Unit 14		
T-Unit 5	*12*	*2*	T-Unit 15		
T-Unit 6	*14*	*2*	T-Unit 16		
T-Unit 7	*16*	*3*	T-Unit 17		
T-Unit 8	*9*	*1*	T-Unit 18		
T-Unit 9	*12*	*2*	T-Unit 19		
T-Unit 10	*17*	*2*	T-Unit 20		
Total Words (A)			*146*		
Total Clauses (B)			22		
Total T-Units (C)			*11*		
Mean Words Per Clause (A/B)			6.6		
Mean Clauses Per T-Unit (B/C)			2.0		
Mean Words Per T-Unit (A/C)			*13.2*		

Table 3.9 identifies the rating schedule of the expository writing tasks for the three experimental classes, the three control classes, the nine writing tasks (including the pretest), and the schedule by which the three raters assessed the tasks. As can be seen from Table 3.9, each rater read four sets of each assignment. During the experimental period, each rater evaluated each section six times. Consequently, the assessment task is distributed equally among the three possible combination of raters (AC, AB, and BC). The holistic score as well as each analytic subscale score for each task that will be used for the analysis of effects in this study mean assessment of the two raters on the pretest and the posttest separately. For both the analytic and holistic measures, interrater reliability will be established by repeated measures analysis of variance as described by Kelinger (1986). This ANOVA will be a group by occasion by class (2x9x3) design.

Table 3.9. Rating Schedule of Expository Writing Tasks

Writing Assignment	Experimental Group			Control Group		
	1	2	3	1	2	3
Pretest 1	4-5	5-1	3-6	1-2	2-3	6-4
2	5-4	6-1	1-3	2-6	3-5	4-2
3	6-5	1-4	2-1	3-6	4-3	5-2
4	1-2	2-3	3-6	4-5	5-1	6-4
5	2-6	3-5	4-3	5-2	6-1	1-4
6	3-4	4-2	5-6	6-5	1-3	2-1
7	4-2	5-1	6-5	1-3	2-6	3-4
8	5-4	6-1	1-2	2-3	3-6	4-5
Posttest 9	6-1	1-4	2-3	3-5	4-6	5-2

**Codes: 1=First rater, 2=Second rater, 3=Third rater, 4=Fourth rater,
5=Fifth rater, 6=Sixth rater Note: The average of the two raters for each
student will be used for repeated measures ANOVA to establish reliability.**

Table 3.10 illustrates the form that each rater will use for the holistic
and analytic assessments. Cooper (1977) established the reliability of
holistic scales, among them the 4-point scale that the present study will
use. The reliability and validity of an analytic instrument in measuring
aspects of writing was established by Diederich (1966). This instrument
has six subscales or factors that represent the major differences in
qualified readers' assessment of writing. The six factors are: main ideas,
details, organization, cohesion, sentence structure, and usage.
Diederich, French, and Carlton (1961) identified their factors and
established their predictive validity.

During rater training sessions prior to the experiment, convergent-
discriminant validity will be established for the six factors using the
multitrait-multimethod analysis described by Campbell and Fiske (1959).
In this study, the six subscales identified in Table 3.10 were the multiple
traits, and the six raters identified in Table 3.9 were the multiple
"methods."

Rater training was modeled after the procedure described by
Diederich (1966). Three training sessions were scheduled prior to the
experimental period. During the first meeting, the definition of each
subscale factor was discussed with the raters. The raters were
encouraged to describe the distinguishing components of each trait.

Table 3.10. Raters' Instrument for Assessing the Analytic and Holistic
Variables of Nine Expository Writing Tasks

Student_____Section_____Assignment_____

Criterion	Description	Rating
Main Ideas	The degree to which the important ideas are clearly and concisely stated.	
Details	The degree to which relevant information supports the main idea.	
Organization	The degree to which the macro or global structure is logical and coherent.	
Cohesion	The degree to which adjoining sentences are logically connected.	
Sentence Structure	The degree to which sentence structures vary.	
Usage	The degree to which the conventions of Standard English are observed.	
Overall Quality	The degree to which the composition is effective, based on preceding criteria	

Four-point rating criteria: 4=Exemplary, clearly above average although not
necessarily flawless; 3=Good, but sufficiently weak to set it apart from
exemplary work; 2=Average to slightly below average; flawed but acceptable;
1=Clearly below average with serious flaws.

Next, the raters focused on one trait at a time and discussed how it
qualitatively differed in the range of performance typical of ninth-grade
writers. Finally during the session, each rater read and assessed copies
of four pretest essays written by members of the current tenth-grade
class at the school. The four essays, previously evaluated by the three
high school English teachers trained in both holistic and analytic
assessment, modeled the range of performance on the analytic and
holistic variable. The assessments were highly reliable and presumed
valid. After each rater evaluated each of the four essays, the

assessments were compared and discussed to identify aberrant raters and to begin the process of changing their assessment style.

During the second training session, the raters examined the experimental materials and discussed the eight discourse functions. The raters reviewed exemplary expository writing models of each discourse function, taken from the answer section of the experimental materials. Finally, the raters assessed four pretests written by members of the current tenth-grade class. The assessments were again compared during the session to identify aberrant raters and to continue the process of changing their assessment style.

The third and final training session began with the assessment of four previously evaluated pretests. Again, the assessments were compared to identify any aberrant raters to continue the process of changing their assessment style. The raters then assessed twelve pretests randomly selected from those written by the current tenth-grade class. Individual conferences were scheduled between the investigator and raters whose scores on any measure remained aberrant. Diederich (1966) observed that these conferences are probably the most effective training that can be given in the use of the rating scale.

Analysis

Pre-analysis of the data checked the assumptions which support the main analysis. Since multivariate analysis of variance (MANOVA) was used in the main analysis, the pre-analysis checked the assumed randomization of subject assignment as well as the normalcy of the distribution and the equivalence of the standard deviations of all pretest, interim, and posttest measures. Correlation analysis revealed whether the correlation between the variables measured during the pretest, interim, and posttest periods were significant and linear. Factor analysis of the same variables revealed their structure; that is, the extent to which they were similarly affected by the independent variable and may be clustered in the analysis. Based on the results of the pre-analysis, adjustments would have been made to the analysis plan if necessary. None were necessary. In this study, the main analysis would have shifted for MANOVA to multivariate analysis of covariance (MANCOVA) if necessary.

Repeated measures MANOVA was used for the main analysis in this study because it is well adapted to testing fairly complex theoretical formulations, since their very nature is the analysis of several variables at once. In this study, the repeated measures MANOVA approach analyzed, at one time, the holistic, analytic, and syntactic variables for pretest-posttest change. Despite the fact that noteworthy sentence-combining studies like that of Kerek et al (1980) used analysis of covariance for their main analyses, the MANOVA approach was selected for this study because, as Kerlinger (1986) asserts, analysis of covariance is simply not well suited to exploratory factor analysis or to testing mean differences between groups or subgroups of data. If it is possible to use a simpler procedure like analysis of variance and obtain answers to research questions, Kerlinger (1986) concluded, then using analysis of covariance is pointless.

Repeated measures MANOVA with trend analysis was used for the secondary analysis of the data to discover any pattern of change, in relation to the expected change, across the syntactic, analytic, and holistic variables during the experimental period. Table 3.11 predicted that difficulty of ninth-grade students of average reading and writing ability in their attempt (1) to comprehend the ideas on which the writing assignments are based and (2) to perform the exposition writing tasks. These predictions, based on the varying complexity of the ideas and writing tasks, helped to explain non-linear trends in the students' written performance throughout the experimental period. Finally, the secondary analysis established correlations between students' performances on (1) the mapping and cued sentence-combining tests and (2) the posttest variables. It should be noted that once it was established empirically that

Table 3.11. Difficulty Ratings: Anticipated Ability of Students to Comprehend Ideas and to Perform Expository Writing Tasks.

Difficulty of Writing Tasks	Difficulty of Ideas		
	Very Difficult	Moderately Difficult	Minimally Difficult
Very Difficult			
Moderatly Difficult	2, 3, 4, 7	8	6
Minimally Difficult	5	1	P

Cell codes: Numbers=Writing tasks (1-8) assigned during 8-week experimental period. P=Pretest.

subjects had indeed been randomly assigned to groups, posttest-only analyses were all that needed to be done with the exception of the trend analysis, and the pretest was used to block students into high, medium, and low ability group for analysis.

Summary

The present study investigated the influence of discourse-function sentence combining on the expository writing of ninth graders. The independent variable was sentence-combining activities consisting of both cued and open exercises. The treatment was divided into eight units, each of which was organized around discourse strategies adapted from Pitkin (1977). The two dependent variables investigated in this study were writing quality and syntactic maturity. The writing quality of the pretest expository writing tasks administered during the experimental period was measured in two ways. First, the overall quality of the subjects' performance was judged by three experienced high-school English teachers using a 4-point holistic instrument. In addition, writing quality was assessed by six experienced high-school English teachers with an analytic instrument whose criteria were: organization, main ideas, details, cohesion, sentence structure, and usage. Syntactic maturity was measured in the manner described by Hunt (1965). In the present investigation, the measure that comprised this variable include: words per T-unit, words per clause, and clause per T-unit.

The present study was conducted in a suburban regional technical high school located in the Northeastern region of the United States. The five towns comprising the region have an aggregate population of 119,000 and are primarily middle-class . Ninety-five percent of the regional population are white.   Approximately 120 ninth-grades students. 80 males and 40 females, participated in the study.   These students, who comprised the entire 4-level population of ninth-grade English students at the school, were judged of average to low-average verbal ability based on their performance on (1) the "Reading Comprehension" subtest of the <u>Stanford Diagnostic Reading Test</u> (<u>SDRT</u>), 1985, Blue Level, Form G and (2) the <u>Shawsheen Writing Test</u>, Form B.

For the holistic and analytic ratings of writing effectiveness, as well as for the three factors of syntactic maturity, a pretest-posttest control group design was used. Both the pretest and posttest were expository writing tasks whose validity was established in the manner described in the Instrumentation section of this chapter. Both writing tasks elicit similar (comparison/contrast) responses from the students. The pretest was administered to all eighth-grade applicants to the school as the composition component of the school's battery of placement tests between May and August preceding their admission. The posttest was the last of eight expository writing tasks assigned to all experimental and control students during the experimental period. In addition to the pretest-posttest comparison, all interim writing tasks were assessed with the same instruments to measure any treatment-by-discourse-function interactions.

In the attempt to control confounding variables associated with intrasession history and other factors, instructional units for both the experimental and control groups began with the semantic mapping exercises which reviewed the biology content on which the expository writing tasks were based. The mapping activities also ensured that all students were prepared to write in a similar fashion and that observed differences in writing were not primarily due to differences in preparation to write, but rather due to the treatment and variables examined in this study.

Following the mapping exercise, each of the eight lessons provided practice in both cued and open sentence-combining activity. Cued sentence combining is an individual component of a complex skill.

Open sentence-combining exercises immediately followed the cued activity. Open sentence-combining is an instructional technique that involves the fading of the cues around which the preceding exercises were structured.

Each of the eight instructional units concluded with one expository writing exercise. The expository writing exercises eliminated all syntactic cues and provided no pre-written text.

At the end of each week, two tests were administered to measure the students' knowledge of (1) the organization of the biology content as presented in their texts and (2) the discourse strategy. Students' scores were recorded each week and across the treatment period to assess the correlation of each (map and sentence-combining) measure to the dependent variables.

The control students began each week with identical mapping exercises. However, they were subsequently engaged in traditional syntax activity. At the conclusion of each week, the control students were administered mapping tests and expository writing exercises identical to those assigned to the experimental students. In addition to these measures, the control students were administered traditional syntax-knowledge tests.

The assessment of each expository writing task occurred in three phases. The first phase began on Friday of the academic week and ended on Monday of the shop week. During that 4-day period, the syntactic variables were measured by six English teachers. The second assessment phase occurred between Tuesday and Thursday of the shop week. The third assessment phase occurred between the ensuing Friday and Sunday. During each of these phases, each writing task was assessed analytically and holistically by one of three raters.

Pre-analysis of the data checked the assumptions which support the main analysis. Since multivariate analysis of variance (MANOVA) was used in the main analysis, the pre-analysis checked the assumed randomization of subject assignment as well as the normalcy of the distribution and the equivalence of the standard deviations of all pretest, interim, and posttest measures. Correlation analysis revealed whether the correlations between the variables measured during the pretest, interim, and posttest periods was linear. Factor analysis of the same variables revealed their structure; that is, the extent to which they were similarly affected by the independent variable and the extent to which they could be clustered in the analysis. Based on the results of the pre-analysis, adjustments would have been made to the analysis plan if necessary. None were necessary. In this study, the main analysis would have shifted from MANOVA to analysis of covariance if necessary.

Repeated measures MANOVA with trend analysis was used for the secondary analysis of the data to discover any pattern of change, in relation to the expected change, across the syntactic, analytic, and holistic variables during the experimental period. Finally, the secondary analysis established correlations between students' performances on (1) the mapping and cued sentence-combining tests and (2) the posttest variables.

CHAPTER 4

ANALYSIS OF DATA

The purpose of this study was the investigation of the effects of a discourse-function sentence-combining treatment on two dependent variables, the syntactic maturity and the quality of the expository writing of ninth graders. Syntactic maturity was measured by the calculation of word per T-unit, clauses per T-unit, and words per clause in the manner prescribed by Hunt (1965.) Writing quality was assessed with an analytic instrument whose criteria were: organization, main ideas, details, cohesion, sentence structure, and usage. Finally, the overall quality of the subjects' performance was judged with a 4-point holistic instrument. The research questions focused on how a discourse-function sentence-combining treatment affects measures of ninth graders' performance on each syntactic, analytic, and holistic variables.

The Main Analysis

Repeated measures MANOVA was used for the main analysis in this study because it is well adapted to testing the fairly complex theoretical formulations of this study. The syntactic, analytic, and holistic variables of this study were analyzed for pretest-posttest change simultaneously by a repeated measures MANOVA analysis.

Table 4.1. Summary of MANOVA comparison of Pretest and Posttest Experimental (E) and Control (C) Group Means and Variances.

Variable	Pretest means	Posttest means	Pretest variances	Posttest variances
Mean words/ clause	NS	E>C, p=0.08	E>C	NS
Mean clauses/T-unit	NS	E>C, p=0.03	NS	E>C
Mean words/T-unit	NS	E>C, p=0.00	NS	E>C
Main ideas	NS	E>C, p=0.00	NS	NS
Details	NS	E>C, p=0.00	NS	NS
Organization	NS	E>C, p=0.00	NS	NS
Cohesion	NS	E>C, p=0.03	NS	NS
Sentence Structure	NS	E>C, p=0.05	NS	NS
Usage	NS	E>C, p=0.00	NS	NS
Overall Quality	NS	E>C, p=0.00	NS	NS

NS=Not significant at the 0.05 level.

Table 4.1 presents a summary comparison of the pretest and posttest means and variances for the experimental and control groups. The overall multivariate F was highly significant at the $p<.0001$ level. As can be seen from the table, the differences in pretest-posttest mean scores of the experimental group on main ideas, details, sentence structure, usage, and overall quality were significantly greater than those of the control group.   The table also reveals that the experimental group's posttest variances on two syntactic measures, mean clauses per T-unit and words per T-unit, were greater than those of the control group.   The experimental group's increased posttest variance can be explained by the types of syntactic structures modeled in the treatment's cued sentence-combining exercises. Because only one of the thirteen modeled structures was clausal, the experimental group used various types of phrases to accommodate specific discourse objectives during the treatment period. As a result, the relative infrequency of the experimental group's exposure to clausal structures appears to have negatively influenced the mean number of clauses per T-unit and, consequently, the mean number of words per T-unit.

Table 4.2. An Analysis of Pretest and Posttest Variance Differences Using Hartley's Fmax Statistic

Variable	Hartley's Fmax statistic	
	Pretest	Posttest
Mean words per clause	2.88	1.25
Mean clauses per T-unit	1.56	7.43*
Mean words per T-unit	1.36	2.86*
Main ideas	1.42	1.16
Details	1.09	1.08
Organization	1.35	1.03
Cohesion	1.28	1.18
Sentence structure	1.29	1.49
Usage	1.08	1.84
Overall quality	1.27	1.07

*Indicates a significant difference in variance between groups at the 0.05 level.

Table 4.2 presents the pretest and posttest variance differences of the experimental and control groups using Hartley's Fmax statistic. The Fmax statistic is the larger of the two variances divided by the smaller, where the variance is the square of the standard deviation. As can be seen from the table, only the posttest variance difference for mean clauses per T-unit and mean words per T-unit were significant at the 0.05 level. The experimental group's larger posttest variance can be attributed to the effects of the sentence-combining treatment which modeled thirteen discrete syntactic structures (see Table 3.5) One of the thirteen structures modeled dependent clauses; six modeled various phrases; four modeled compounded elements; and two modeled single-word elements. Since the sentence structure in compositions written by the experimental subjects was significantly more varied than that of the control group from pretest to posttest, the greater variance observed in these two syntactic variables is a consistent effect.

Mean Number of Words per Clause

The observed mean words per clause for both groups increased from the pretest to the posttest. Although the increase was greater for the experimental group (1.68) than for the control group (1.35), the increase was not found to be significantly different between groups. Given the sample size in this study and the somewhat low observed reliability levels, which most affects the difference scores (as this random "noise" is added twice to the difference score), small effects are very difficult to detect statistically in this study. The observed increases, however, are consistent with the findings of Hunt (1965a,b), whose data suggested that, among the syntactic ratios devised in his seminal study, words per clause was the measure most likely to increase as a result of writing treatment.

Mean Number of Clauses per T-Unit

The observed mean number of clauses per T-unit for both groups decreased from the pretest to the posttest. Although the decrease was greater for the control group (-0.718) than for the experimental group (-0.507), the decrease was not found to be significantly different between groups (F=0.92). The decline within the experimental group can be explained by the types of syntactic structures modeled by the cued exercises. Of these 13 structures identified in Table 3.5 of this study, only one is clausal. The rest of the constructions are various types of phrases. Thus, the relative infrequency of the experimental group's exposure to clausal structures appears to have negatively influenced the mean number of clauses written during the treatment period.

For both groups, the discourse mode of the posttest writing task also appears to have negatively influenced this measure. Discourse mode (i.e. narration, description, exposition, and argumentation) affects the syntactic parameters of writing (Mellon, 1969; San Jose, 1972; Crowhurst, 1977). In particular, clauses per t-unit tends to increase in narratives but not in exposition (Green, 1972.) Because the pretest writing task was a narrative but the posttest task was exposition, the posttest decline of both groups may be attributed to the difference in discourse mode, as exposition is the more difficult task for high school students.

Mean Number of Words per T-Unit

The mean number of words per T-unit for both groups decreased from pretest to posttest, as did the mean number of clauses per t-unit,. The decrease was greater for the control group (-3.252) than for the experimental group (-0.699). A large significant difference (F=10.7, p<.001) was observed between the experimental and control groups on their ability to write in an expository manner. The experimental group was better able to handle expository writing, by a wider margin, than the control group. As in clauses per t-unit, the posttest measure of this syntactic variable seems to have been affected by the expository posttest writing task.

Analytic Assessment of Main Ideas

The observed mean analytic assessment of main ideas increased for the experimental group from the pretest to the posttest (+0.125) and decreased for the control group (-0.262). The difference scores between groups was enough to be significant at the 0.05 level of significance. A large significant difference (F=14.1, p<.001) was observed between the experimental and control groups on their ability to write in an expository manner. The experimental group was better able to handle expository writing, by a wider margin, than the control group. The main ideas in compositions written by the experimental subjects were significantly more clearly expressed than those of the control group from pretest to posttest.

Analytic Assessment of Details

The observed mean analytic assessment of details increased for the experimental group from the pretest to the posttest (+0.214) and decreased for the control group (-0.274), as did the observed mean analytic assessments of main ideas. The pretest-posttest difference between groups was significant at the 0.01 level (F=6.51. A large significant difference (F=18.0, p<.001) was observed between the experimental and control groups on their ability to write in an expository manner. The experimental group was better able to handle expository writing, by a wider margin, than the control group. The details in compositions written by the experimental subjects were significantly more relevant to the main ideas and more sufficient in number than those of the control group from pretest to posttest.

Analytic Assessment of Organization

The observed mean analytic assessment of organization for both groups decreased from the pretest to the posttest. The decrease was significantly greater (F=10.1, p,.001) for the control group (-0.274) than for the experimental group (-0.036), and again the caveats about the difference scores stated under *Mean Number of Words per Clause* apply here, once again making the posttest differences the more valid analysis and indication of effects.

Analytic Assessment of Cohesion

The observed mean analytic assessment of cohesion for both groups decreased from pretest to posttest, as did the organization measure. The decrease was greater in the control group (-0.286) than in the experimental group (-0.134), at the .03 level (F=4.77). The unfamiliar posttest topic likely influenced the posttest decline of both groups, whose naïvete in response to a comparison of the male and female reproductive systems negatively affected both the content and the cohesive links of the essays.

Analytic Assessment of Sentence Structure

The observed mean analytic assessment of sentence structure significantly increased (F=4.1, p<.05) for the experimental group from the pretest to the posttest (+0.152) and decreased for the control group (-0.167). As with Main Ideas and Details, the difference scores between groups was also significant at the 0.05 level. The sentence structure in compositions written by the experimental subjects was significantly more varied than that of the control group from pretest to posttest.

Analytic Assessment of Usage

The observed mean analytic assessment of usage increased for the experimental group from the pretest to the posttest (+0.214) and decreased for the control group (-0.321). The difference between groups was significant (F=11.3, p<.001), as it was with Main Ideas, Details, and Sentence Structure.   The syntactic usage in compositions written by the experimental group was significantly more concise and consistent with the conventions of Standard English than that of the control group from pretest to posttest.

Holistic Assessment of Overall Quality

The observed mean holistic assessment of overall quality increased for the experimental group from the pretest to the posttest (+0.152) and decreased for the control group (-0.310).   The difference between groups was significant (F=11.3, p<.001), as it was with Main Ideas, Details, Sentence Structure, and Usage. The overall quality of the compositions written by the experimental subjects was significantly superior than that of the control group from pretest to posttest.

This particular finding is similar to those of other experiments in which students with sentence-combining experience produced writing judged superior in quality to that produced by control students (Combs, 1975; Pederson, 1977; Schuster, 1976; Waterfall, 1977; and Swan, 1977; Kerek et al., 1980.)   Much of the appeal of sentence-combining practice to researchers and teachers alike, observe Kerek et al. (1980), derives from its demonstrated ability to improve the quality of students' writing.   The instructional approach characteristic of most sentence-combining treatments seems to contribute to this result. This approach, sometimes described as "contextualization," accounts for the effective transfer of syntactic skills into larger chunks of written discourse. Stewart (1978), for example, engaged his classes in an "exploration and evaluation of sentence combining options" and "periodically tested" their acquired techniques "for usefulness in short compositions." Callaghan (1977) gave his students "a chance to decide which syntactic options are most appropriate to the whole piece."   Swan (1978) reported that "in class time was spent evaluating and discussing" the transformations, and that instructors encouraged students "to employ sentence combining techniques in their free-writing and editing." Thus, combining exercises have not been divorced from the broader rhetorical context, conclude Kerek et al (1980), which alone can lend them a sense of semantic naturalness and communicative reality.

The Secondary Analysis

Repeated measures MANOVA with trend analysis was used for the secondary analysis of the data to discover any pattern of change, in relation to expected change (See Table 3.11), across the syntactic, analytic, and holistic variables during the experimental period. Table 4.3 presents a summary comparison of experimental- and control-group means over time along with the identification of the best fitting significant overall trend.. As can be seen from the table, the groups differed significantly at the posttest on nine of the ten measured variables. The trend analyses reveal a sudden decline in the performance of the control group with respect to these variables. Members of the school's Science Department, the content experts who had predicted that all the students would respond to the topic with "moderate

Table 4.3. Summary of Repeated Measure Comparisons of Group Means Over Time.

Variable	Pre	2	3	4	5	6	7	8	Post	Trend
Mean words/clause										Cubic
Mean clauses/T-unit			•	•		•			•	Cubic
Mean words/T-unit			•			•			•	Linear
Main Ideas			•						•	Quartic
Details							•		•	Quartic
Organization			•		•				•	Quartic
Cohesion									•	Quadratic
Sentence Structure			•	•					•	Quadratic
Usage				•			•		•	Quartic
Overall Quality									•	Quartic

• Indicates groups are significantly different at the 0.05 level.

difficulty," were consulted about the decline. After they reviewed the curricula of the experimental and control groups, these teachers indicated that they were not, in fact, surprised by the control group's posttest performance. The posttest writing task required all students to "contrast the male and female reproductive systems." The Science staff indicated that, since ninth graders tend to be particularly uninformed about this topic and since the only pre-writing activity that could enhance the control group's knowledge of the topic was a brief mapping exercise, naïve responses and the posttest decline were virtual certainties. In retrospect, the selection of posttest topics appears inappropriate or at least problematic. Additionally, social desirability as well as religious and other background factors might also have inhibited responses among the control-group students.

Mean Words Per Clause

The observed control-group mean words per clause were less than the experimental means, with the exception of assignment 6. The greatest difference occurring at the posttest. The trend was not found to be significantly different for the groups. As predicted (See Table 3.11), both groups appear to have had moderate difficulty with writing tasks 3, 5, and 8, accounting for the pattern of their performance on this variable. The observed trend best fits a cubic function. ($F=76.9$, $p<.001$)

Mean Clauses Per T-Unit

The observed control-group mean clauses per T-unit were consistently less than the experimental-group means, with the greatest difference occurring at the posttest. The trend for both groups appears to be decreasing overall, but the trend difference between groups was not significant. The observed trend best fits a cubic function ($F=36.0$, $p<.001$)

Mean Words Per T-Unit

The observed mean words per T-unit of the control group were consistently lower than those of the experimental group, as were the means for clauses per T-unit, with the greatest difference occurring at the posttest. The trend appears to be decreasing overall for both groups, but the difference between the groups was not significant. The observed trend best fits a linear function. (F=12.3, p<.001)

Analytic Assessment of Main Ideas

The overall trend for the control group on main ideas appears to be decreasing, while that for the experimental group appears to be increasing. The difference in trend between groups was found to be significant (F=6.4, p<.01). The MANOVA results for pretest-posttest differences indicated that the main ideas written by the experimental group were significantly more clearly expressed than those of the control group. This analysis suggests that the difference in behavior between groups extends to a significant difference in trends over all time periods. As predicted (see Table 3.11), the experimental group appears to have had difficulty with the ideas in writing tasks 3 and 4, while the control group apparently had difficulty with the ideas in tasks 4 and 8, accounting for the pattern of their performance on this variable. The observed trend best fits a quartic function. (F=10.0, p<.001)

Analytic Assessment of Details

The overall trend for the control group on details appears to be decreasing, as it did with main ideas, while that for the experimental group is increasing. The difference in trend between groups is significant (p<.002). The MANOVA results for the pretest-posttest differences showed that the details written by the experimental group were significantly more related to the main ideas and more sufficient in number. This analysis suggests that the difference in behavior between group extends to a significant difference in trends over all time periods. As predicted (see Table 3.11), the experimental group appears to have had difficulty with the ideas in writing tasks 3 and 4, while the control group apparently had difficulty with the ideas in tasks 4 and 8, accounting for the pattern of their performance on this variable. The observed trend best fits a quartic function. (F=9.7, p<.001)

Analytic Assessment of Organization

The overall trend for the control group appears to be decreasing, while that of the experimental group is increasing. Although the difference in trend between groups was significant at the 0.02 level, the test result was not as strong as that for Main Ideas ($p < .005$) or Details ($p < .002$). In addition, there was no significant pretest-posttest difference found between groups. As predicted (see Table 3.11), the experimental group appears to have had difficulty with the ideas in writing tasks 3 and 4, while the control group apparently had difficulty with the ideas in tasks 5 and 8, accounting for the pattern of their performance on this variable. The observed trend best fits a quartic function. ($F = 7.31$, $p < .001$)

Analytic Assessment of Cohesion

The overall trend on cohesion for the control group appears to be decreasing, while that of the experimental group is increasing. As with Organization, the difference in trend between groups was significant at the 0.04 level, but the results were not strong. The MANOVA test for pretest-posttest differences indicated that there was significant posttest difference between groups, and one can see this difference trend emerging in the last three data points. As predicted (see Table 3.11), the experimental group appears to have had difficulty with the ideas in writing tasks 3 and 4, while the control group apparently had difficulty with the ideas in tasks 4, 5, and 8, accounting for the pattern of their performance on this variable. The observed trend best fits a quadratic function.

Analytic Assessment of Sentence Structure

The overall sentence-structure trend appears to be decreasing for the control group and increasing for the experimental group. The difference in trend is significant ($p < 0.003$), as it is with Main Ideas and Details, and with Organization and Cohesion at the 0.05 level. The MANOVA results for pretest-posttest differences indicated significantly more varied sentence structure in the compositions written by the

Experimental group than by those of the Control group.   That difference in behavior between groups extends to a significant difference in trend over the study. As predicted (see Table 3.11), the experimental group appears to have had difficulty with writing tasks 3 and 6, while the control group apparently had difficulty with tasks 4, 6, and 8, accounting for the pattern of their performance on this variable. The observed trend best fits a quadratic function. ($F=4.0$, $p<.05$)

Analytic Assessment of Usage

The overall usage trend appears to be decreasing for the control group and increasing for the experimental group. The difference in trend is significant ($p<0.001$), as it is with Main Ideas, Details, and Sentence Structure, and with Organization and Cohesion at the 0.05 level.   The MANOVA results for pretest-posttest differences indicated that the syntactic usage in compositions written by the experimental group was significantly more concise and consistent with the conventions of Standard English than that of the control group.   That difference in behavior between groups extends to a significant difference in trend over the study. As predicted (Table 3.11), the experimental group appears to have had difficulty with writing tasks 3 and 4, while the control group apparently had difficulty with tasks 4 and 8, accounting for the pattern of their performance on this variable. The observed trend best fits a quartic function. ($F=4.3$, $p<.04$)

Holistic Assessment of Overall Quality

The overall-quality trend appears to be decreasing for the control group and increasing for the experimental group. This difference in trend is significant ($p<0.002$), as it was with Main Ideas, Details, Sentence structure, and Usage, and with Organization and Cohesion at the 0.05 level.   The MANOVA test for pretest-posttest difference indicated that the Overall Quality of the compositions written by the experimental group was significantly superior to that of the control group.   That difference in behavior between groups extends to a significant difference in trend over the study. As predicted (see Table 3.11), the experimental group appears to have had difficulty with tasks 3 and 4, while the control group apparently had difficulty with tasks 4 and 8, accounting for their performance on this variable. The observed trend best fits a quartic function. (F=7.5, p<.01)   Again, the difference between the Experimental and Control groups is emerging in the last three trials, which suggests that the dynamics of the change are at first highly variable but then begin to stabilize and progress systematically.

Summary

In this study, repeated measures MANOVA was used for the main analysis of the dependent variables, which included three syntactic variables, six analytic variables, and one holistic variable. The syntactic variables were: mean words per clause, mean clauses per T-unit, and mean words per T-unit. The analytic variables were: main ideas, details, organization, cohesion, sentence structure, usage, and overall quality. The holistic variable was overall quality. For some of these variables (words per clause, words per T-unit, main ideas, details, and organization), the observed pretest-posttest increase of the experimental group was greater than that of the control group but was not found to be significant, likely because of the sample size and the somewhat low observed reliability levels, which most affect the difference scores as this random "noise" is added twice to the them, making small effects very difficult to detect.

The posttest means of the experimental group on all dependent variables were larger than those of the control group. For both groups, the posttest means for two syntactic variables clauses per T-unit and words per T-unit) and for two analytic variables (organization and cohesion) were smaller than the pretest means. With respect to the syntactic variables, this decrease can be attributed to the effects of the treatment, which modeled few clausal transitions and many phrase structures. With respect to the analytic variables, the posttest decrease can be attributed to the effects of responding to difficult expository text during the treatment period. The experimental group demonstrated fairly large posttest gains on measures of main ideas, details, usage, and overall quality.   These findings support previous studies (O"Hare, 1973; Combs, 1975; Pedersen, 1977; Schuster, 1976; Waterfall, 1977; Swan, 1977; Kerek et al, 1980) which observed rhetorical gains in students who participated in sentence-combining treatments.

Repeated measures MANOVA with trend analysis was used for the secondary analysis of the data to discover any pattern change, in relation to expected change, across the syntactic, analytic, and holistic variables during the experimental period. At the posttest, the groups differed significantly on nine of the ten measured variables. These posttest differences can, in part, be attributed to the factors that might have inhibited control-group students in response to the posttest writing task. However, on the five dependent variables (main ideas, details, sentence structure, usage, and overall quality) for which the experimental group demonstrated significant posttest gains according to the ANOVA analysis, the overall trend for the control group appears to be decreasing, while that for the experimental group appears to be increasing. These analyses suggest that the difference in behavior between groups extends to a significant difference in trends over all time periods.

CHAPTER 5

CONCLUSIONS AND DISCUSSION

Overview

The purpose of our research was to investigate the effects of a discourse-function sentence-combining treatment on measures of the syntactic component and overall writing quality of ninth graders. Hunt's (1965) study of the developmental differences in the written syntax of students and adults spurred many investigations of the effects of sentence combining treatments. Spanning two decades, more than 40 studies varied not only in treatment procedures but also in results. In particular, no conclusive links between treatment and significant growth in overall writing quality were established. Our research, therefore, began by assuming that effects, where present in the literature, were attributable to the treatment's generating in their subjects a sense of text or discourse structure and function. This view was essentially a cognitive view of our findings. Although sentence-combining researchers have acknowledged the importance of such syntax-to-discourse transfer, their treatments achieve it in varying degrees through incidental or vague procedures.

In contrast to these loosely integrated procedures, discourse-function sentence combining is a specific approach first suggested by Suhor (1978), who described rhetorical modes (e.g. comparison, contrast, cause and effect) as discrete cognitive operations and suggested that instruction in syntax should be organized by cognitive operation, rather than by syntactic structure, to effect the rhetorical component of writing. Suhor strongly suggested that a sentence-combining approach to writing instruction, particularly one modeled after Pitkin's (1978) discourse strategies, would bring manipulation of syntax into direct relationship with thinking skills. A sentence-combining approach, he suggested, would promote greater variety and elasticity in the expression of the respective rhetorical modes.

One of the major benefits of our research is its contribution to knowledge pertaining to those sentence-combining treatments which are designed to enhance measures of overall writing quality. The empirical support of our major hypothesis clearly suggests that one explanation for sentence combining's effectiveness as a writing treatment is the application of Pitkin's principles of discourse hierarchy. These results, therefore, should be of particular interest to English teachers seeking a new approach to instruction in syntax as well as to curriculum writers seeking a new method of integrating language, writing, and content-area objectives.

Summary of Findings

For the holistic and analytic ratings of writing effectiveness, as well as for the three factors of syntactic maturity, we used a pretest-posttest control group design. Writing quality was assessed by six experienced high school English teachers with an analytic instrument whose criteria included organization, main ideas, details, cohesion, sentence structure, and usage. Syntactic maturity was also assessed by six experienced high-school English teachers and measured in the manner described by Hunt (1965.) In our research, the measures that comprise this variable include words per T-unit, words per clause, and clauses per T-unit.

Our research was conducted in a suburban regional technical high school located in the Northeastern region of the United States. The five towns comprising the region have an aggregate population of 119,000 and are primarily middle class. Ninety-five percent of the regional population are white. Ninety-eight ninth-grade students, 60 males and 38 females, participated in the study. These students were judged of average to low-average verbal ability based on their performance on (1) the "Reading Comprehension" subtest of the <u>Stanford Diagnostic</u>

Reading Test, 1985, Blue Level, Form G and (2) the Shawsheen Writing Test, Form B.

In an attempt to control confounding variables associated with intrasession history and other factors, instructional units for both the experimental and control groups began with semantic mapping exercises, which reviewed the biology content on which the expository writing tasks were based. The mapping activities also ensured that all students prepared to write in a similar fashion and that observed differences in writing were not due primarily to differences in writing preparation, but rather due to the treatment and variables examined in this study. Following the mapping exercise, each of the eight lessons provided practice in both cued and open sentence-combining activity. Cued sentence combining was an individual component of a complex skill. Open sentence combining was an instructional technique that involves the fading of the cues around which the preceding exercises were structured. Each of the eight instructional units concluded with one expository writing exercise. The expository writing exercises eliminated all syntactic cues. At the end of each week, two tests were administered to measure the students' knowledge of (1) the organization of the biology content as presented in their texts and (2) the discourse strategy. Students' scores were recorded each week and across the treatment period to assess the correlation of each (map and sentence-combining) measure to the dependent variables.

The control students began each week with identical mapping exercises. However, they were subsequently engaged in traditional syntax activity. At the conclusion of each week, the control students were administered mapping tests and expository writing exercises identical to those assigned to the experimental students. In addition to these measures, the control students were administered traditional syntax-knowledge tests.

The assessment of each expository writing task occurred in three phases. The first phase began on Friday of the each exam and continued through the subsequent Monday. During that 4-day period, the syntactic variables were measured by six English teachers. The second assessment phases occurred between Tuesday and Thursday. The third assessment phase occurred between Friday and Sunday. During each of these 3-day phases, each writing task was assessed analytically and holistically by one of six raters.

The pre-analysis of the data checked the assumptions which supported the main analysis. Since multivariate analysis of variance (MANOVA) was used in the main analysis, the pre-analysis checked the assumed randomization of subject assignment as well as the normalcy of the distribution and the equivalence of the standard deviations of all pretest, interim, and posttest measures. Repeated measures MANOVA was used for the main analysis in our research because it is well adapted to testing fairly complex theoretical formulations, since its very nature is the analysis of several variables at once. The repeated measures MANOVA approach analyzed simultaneously the holistic, analytic, and syntactic variables for pretest-posttest change. Despite the fact that noteworthy sentence-combining studies like that of Kerek et al (1980) used analysis of covariance for their main analyses, the MANOVA approach was selected for this study because, as Kerlinger (1986) asserts, analysis of covariance is simply not well suited to exploratory analyses or to testing mean differences between groups or subgroups of data. Repeated measures MANOVA with trend analysis was used for the secondary analysis of the data to discover any pattern of change, in relation to the expected change, across the syntactic, analytic, and holistic variables during the experimental period.

The syntactic variables we examined were: mean words per clause, mean clauses per T-unit, and mean words per T-unit. The analytic variables we examined were: main ideas, details, organization, cohesion, sentence structure, usage, and overall quality. The holistic variable we examined was overall quality. For some of these variables (words per clause, words per T-unit, main ideas, details, and organization), the observed pretest-posttest increase of the experimental group was greater than that of the control group but was not found to be significant. This result was most likely due to the sample size and the somewhat low observed reliability levels, which most affect the difference scores, as this random "noise" is added twice to the them, making small effects very difficult to detect.

The posttest means of the experimental group on all dependent variables were larger than those of the control group. For both groups, the posttest means for two syntactic variables (clauses per T-unit and words per T-unit) and for two analytic variables (organization and cohesion) were smaller than the pretest means. With respect to the syntactic variables, this decrease can be attributed to the effects of the treatment, which modeled few clausal transitions and many phrase structures. With respect to the analytic variables, the posttest decrease can be attributed to the effects of responding to difficult expository text during the treatment period. The experimental group demonstrated fairly large posttest gains on measures of main ideas, details, usage, and overall quality.

Repeated measures MANOVA with trend analysis was used for the secondary analysis of the data to discover any pattern change, in relation to expected change, across the syntactic, analytic, and holistic variables during the experimental period. At the posttest, the groups differed significantly on nine of the ten measured variables. These posttest differences can, in part, be attributed to the factors that might have inhibited control-group students in response to the posttest writing task. However, on the five dependent variables (main ideas, details, sentence structure, usage, and overall quality) for which the experimental group demonstrated significant posttest gains according to the ANOVA analysis, the overall trend for the control group appeared to be decreasing, while that for the experimental group appeared to be increasing. These analyses suggest that the difference in behavior between groups extends to a significant difference in trends over all time periods.

These findings support previous studies which observed rhetorical gains in students who participated in sentence-combining treatments. In an early study, O'Hare (1973) concluded that sentence-combining practice is *inherently rhetorical* after his experimental group wrote posttest compositions that were judged significantly better than those of the control group. Further, like the present study, Waterfall's investigation (1977) found that the sentence-combining students gained significant posttest superiority in writing quality but not in syntactic fluency. Similarly, Pedersen (1977) found that although his experimental students achieved only minimal gains in syntactic fluency, their sentence-combining practice influenced numerous qualitative factors, thus exerting "profound influence upon the general cognitive performance" of students in writing. Like the previous studies and the present investigation, Swan (1978) reported that her sentence-combining group wrote longer clauses and improved the quality of their posttest writing. Despite these results, Swan remained guarded, warning that a cause-and-effect relationship between the sentence-combining instruction and improvement in overall writing quality should not necessarily be drawn.

Kerek et al (1980) responded to the type of skepticism articulated by Swan by devising a program that connected sentence-combining practice to specific rhetorical functions. The present study emulates this rhetorical approach, and added to it the discourse functions identified by Pitkin (1978). Kerek at al (1980) observed not only that rhetorically-based sentence-combining practice had a positive effect on overall writing quality, but also that these gains were sustained over 28 months following the experimental period. In addition, these researchers concluded that there seemed to be no direct connection between students' scores on syntactic maturity and their holistic ratings, which was the single most reliable measure of overall writing quality in the study. Similarly, the present investigation could not find any connection or relationship between students' syntactic and holistic scores. Kerek et al (1980), however, did suggest a more likely link between the treatment and writing gains. Cued exercises, these researchers observed, help students to learn sentence patterns that they were later encouraged to use in whole-discourse exercises. The whole-discourse exercises offered a specific context for a series of rhetorical decisions. Students became aware of their options and were able to evaluate the relative effectiveness of each option again within a rhetorical context. In psychological schema theory, (Ashcraft, 1994), this process would be representative of schema instantiation coupled with guided decision making. Thus, Kerek et al (1980) not only responded to the skepticism of researchers like Swan by identifying the critical rhetorical connection between sentence-combining practice and observed gains in students' overall writing quality, but they also predicted the results observed in our research and provided a framework for interpreting such results. This framework will be utilized in the discussion of findings presented below.

Conclusions and Discussion

The analysis of data did not confirm the first hypothesis of our research. The syntactic maturity of the expository compositions written by the experimental students was not found to be significantly higher than those written by the control students. Of the three syntactic variables, posttest growth among both experimental and control students was observed only in Words per Clause (WPC). The increase was greater for the experimental group than for the control group, but the between-groups difference was not significant. The non-significant finding might be attributed to the sample size along with the somewhat low reliability levels in this study, which most affect the difference scores (as this "noise" is added twice to the difference scores), making small effects very difficult to detect. However, the observed posttest increase in WPC is consistent with the findings of Hunt (1965a,b), whose data suggested that, among the syntactic ratios devised in his seminal study, WPC was the measure most likely to increase as a result of sentence-combining practice.

The posttest scores of both the experimental and control groups on the two other syntactic variables, Clauses per T-Unit (CPT) and Words per T-Unit (WPT), were smaller than the pretest scores. This finding is not unique in sentence-combining research. Green (1972), Ney (1976), and Waterfall (1977) reported adverse effects on measures of syntactic maturity as a result of sentence-combining practice. This evidence, however, must be considered alongside the pretest-posttest comparison of both groups on Sentence Structure, one analytic measure of writing quality. The observed mean analytic assessment of Sentence Structure significantly increased for the experimental group from the pretest to the posttest and decreased for the control group. This result indicates that the Sentence Structure of the expository compositions written by the experimental subjects was judged significantly more varied than that of the expository compositions written by the control subjects.

The assumption that gains in writing quality must initiate with syntactic growth is not supported by the overall weight of evidence in our research. In addition to Sentence Structure, the qualitative assessment of compositions in our study was based on five other analytic variables, consisting of Main Ideas, Details, Organization, Coherence, and Usage. Each composition was also rated holistically for Overall Quality. Despite the absence of significant growth (WPC, CPT, WPT) or significant between-group difference (WPC, CPT) on posttest measures of the syntactic variables, the analysis of the data revealed significant between-group posttest differences in *each* analytic and holistic variable. Each of the respective hypotheses, which predicted significantly superior posttest performance by the experimental group on each analytic and holistic measure, was thus confirmed.

These findings support those of previous studies (Pedersen, 1977; Waterfall, 1977), in which the effects of sentence-combining treatments on students' writing were observed directly in the writing quality itself, and not through the mediation of gains in syntactic fluency. The findings of our study also support the observation of Kerek et al (1980) who noted that the hypothesized direct link from syntactic fluency increases to gains in writing quality lacks the support of convincing empirical evidence. It is true that several experiments beginning with O'Hare have shown significant positive influence on both syntactic and writing-quality variables and that from such parallel, concurrent gains it is often (erroneously) concluded that growth in syntactic fluency brings about writing-quality effects. Further, this "syntax-first" view and practice is deeply rooted in theory about sentence combining. But, as Kerek et al (1980) concluded, this view and practice are based more on conjecture than fact, which is exactly what our research has convincingly shown. The considerable and detailed evidence of our study did not support the "syntax-first" view and practice and, in fact, supported precisely the opposite view.

At a more general level, our research has shown that structure, form, and organization or schemas in the psychological sense of the term are critically important in controlling attention and perception and driving the processing of information and in the generation of responses and response alternatives in working memory. What our research has shown is that micro schemas exist and act as micro control devices in evaluative reading and writing processes. Our research has also shown that focusing on building micro control schemas (or micro repertoires) can and does improve the writing performances of adolescents.

This idea of micro schemas, as opposed to macro structures, was formally introduced in the "language" research area by van Dijk in the early eighties (See van Dijk & Kintsch, 1983 and Westphal, 1991), but several aspects of the idea were inherent in Chomsky's model of "surface and deep" structure of both transmission code and meaning (See Chomsky, 1985). In the van Dijk model, rhetorical context would be the macro schema (or structure of created meaning) and our sentence combining techniques would be the micro schema (or micro control devices). The idea of micro control devices comes directly from the field of artificial intelligence.

In artificial intelligence during the past decade, the view of the "large all encompassing program" that is "intelligence" or "the mind" has proven to be an inoperable concept and has been abandoned for the view of a "fuzzy macro program" that is loosely connected to repertoires of "small programs" or "micro control devices" that work fairly independently and in parallel to solve "local" problems and handle processing (Franklin, 1995). These "small programs" or micro control devices are called "insect intelligence" in the flamboyant rhetoric of the AI community. Insect intelligence is currently very "hot" and the guiding idea for many craft exploring Mars and other planets. What this new view in AI shows is that many seemingly competing ideas are not necessarily "either/or" but may indeed be "both/and." The ideas of macro and micro schemas and control devices are a concrete example of this point as it applies to language and writing and the understanding and teaching of both these phenomena. In addition, this point and our findings show the critical importance of the "response generation" component in our information processing model and theory of learning (See Carifio, 1993). Chomsky was one of the first theorists to truly distinguish between competence and performance (See Chomsky, 1985). He stressed that performance (writing) problems may not necessarily be an indication of a lack of competence (knowledge and understanding). Rather, they may due to a lack of skills and/or a lack of concerted effort to explicitly develop the skills that are necessary to express the competence that exists. Chomsky's view perfectly expresses why we are so interested in sentence-combining techniques and the degree to which mastery of these techniques would improve the writing of adolescents. Our research has shown that making the effort to build the response generation component has real payoffs and that there is much to be gained in building students' micro control schemas and repertoires.

Next Steps

The trend analyses reveal that, for the most part, the difference in the performance of the Experimental and Control groups was emerging in the last three trials. This pattern suggests that the dynamics of the change are at first highly variable but then begin to stabilize and progress systematically. However, the trend analyses additionally reveal precipitous posttest declines in the performance of the control group on most variables. Members of the school's Science Department, the content experts who had predicted that all the students would respond to the posttest writing topic with "moderate difficulty," were consulted about the decline. After they reviewed the curricula of the experimental and control groups, these teachers indicated that they were not, in fact, surprised by the control group's posttest performance. The posttest writing task required all students to "contrast the male and female reproductive systems." The Science staff indicated that, since ninth graders tend to be particularly uninformed about this topic and since the only pre-writing activity that could enhance the control group's knowledge of the topic was a brief mapping exercise, naïve responses and the posttest decline were virtual certainties. In retrospect, the selection of posttest topics appears inappropriate or at least problematic. Additionally, social desirability as well as religious and other background factors might also have inhibited responses among the control-group students. Subsequent investigators should assess their writing topics in terms of these potentially confounding variables, namely students' naivete as well as their religious or social inhibitions, and choose more neutral and age appropriate topics for students' expository essays.

The selection of the pretest topic also proved to be a problem. The topic was selected because of its structural similarity to the planned posttest. Both were contrast tasks. The pretest required the students to contrast effective and ineffective teachers and teaching styles. The posttest, as previously discussed, prompted a contrast of the male and female reproductive systems. Although the assignments were similar in terms of this discourse structure, they differed considerably in terms of technical content. The pretest, for many students, was treated like a memoir. The content flowed like narrative as students recalled and dutifully contrasted their fond and less-than-fond interactions with teachers. On the other hand, the posttest was much more expository in nature, requiring students to recall and structure (often unfamiliar) scientific knowledge. Further research should consider not only the rhetorical or discourse structure of the writing tasks but also the degree of technical or scientific prior knowledge required by the students to respond completely and effectively to the respective assignments.

A final problematic area in the present investigation was interrater reliability. The procedure described by Diederich (1966) appeared sufficient, but later proved otherwise. In our study, three training sessions were scheduled prior to the experimental period. During the first session, the definition of each subscale factor was discussed, and the raters were encouraged to describe the distinguishing components of each trait. In addition, the raters discussed how each trait qualitatively differs in the range of performance typical of ninth graders. Finally, the raters read and assessed four essays which had been previously evaluated by three high-school English teachers trained in both holistic and analytic assessment. The essays represented the range of performance on the analytic and holistic variables. Aberrant raters were identified, and conferences were held to change their assessment style.

During the second training session, the raters examined the experimental materials and discussed the eight discourse functions. The raters reviewed exemplary expository writing models of each discourse function, taken from the answer section of the experimental materials. Finally, the raters assessed four previously evaluated pretests written by members of the (then) tenth-grade class at the experimental site. Again, the essays were selected for their qualitative diversity, and again aberrant assessments were discussed. During the third session, the raters assessed twelve previously evaluated pretests that had been randomly selected from those written by the same tenth-grade class. By this time, aberrant assessments were minimal, and it appeared that convergent-discriminant validity had been firmly established.

Thus, at the beginning of the experimental period, the raters' assessments of the respective variables were similar. However, despite this training, their convergence began to wane not long after. The somewhat low observed reliability levels suggest that the training approach would benefit from modification. To check this drift among raters, it is recommended that review sessions be scheduled during the experimental period. In the case of the present 16-week study, it would not be unreasonable to schedule review sessions at 4-week intervals. During these reviews, activities like those described in the previous sessions might be conducted in order to prevent raters – particularly those with many years of teaching experience – from reverting to old, idiosyncratic styles of assessment.

Further research into the effects of sentence-combining practice on the syntactic and rhetorical characteristics of written composition should continue to investigate the treatments' effects on the syntactic variables identified by Hunt (1965). To be sure, further evidence is needed not only to understand what types of sentence-combining activity positively affect these variables but also to observe how rhetorical variables are impacted by the presence or absence of these gains. Most critically, however, further research must continue to explore the effects of sentence-combining treatments on various rhetorical or discourse objectives. Investigators should continue to pay attention to chunks of texts of varying length.   Kerek et al (1980) are quite correct in recommending carefully modeled whole-discourse exercises as the focus of subsequent study, but that is not to say that sentence-length exercises, like those devised by Mellon (1969) and used in part in the present study, are no longer useful components of sentence-combining practice.   How classroom teachers can concretely utilize the findings of our research and the prototypical examples of instructional materials and exercises we developed is given in the next chapter.

A Brief Afterword

It is our considered opinion that John Mellon simply must relent.   In 1969, Mellon argued that the exclusive objective of sentence-combining practice is the enhancement of syntactic fluency in English composition. He aggressively defended the treatment's a-rhetorical character.   Ten years later, in response to a mounting body of research yielding convincing evidence that sentence-combining practice was positively affecting the overall quality of students' writing, Mellon (1979) proclaimed that large syntactic-fluency increases must inevitably, sooner or later, boost quality scores.   He added, however, and with typical disdain, that the concern for immediate over-all quality improvement is a turning away from serious writing research.

More recently, Mellon's theoretical whimsy has steered him toward serious esoterica.   Daiker et al (1985), in apparent deference to sentence-combining's pre-eminent investigator and writer, included Mellon's "The Role of the Elaborated Dominant Nominal (EDN) in the Measurement of Conceptual and Syntactic Fluencies in Expository Writing" as the introductory piece in their anthology (ironically) titled Sentence Combining: A Rhetorical Perspective.   In his discussion, Mellon steadfastly maintains that those competencies from which overall writing quality emerges are syntactic skills.   He further suggests that these EDN's – which can be simply defined as nonembedded noun clauses – reflect a language production variable that might be called "conceptual fluency."   In a rare moment of self-deprecation, Mellon observes in his article that Lester Faigley characterized conceptual fluency as a term in search of a concept.   Mellon, of course, proceeded to define the construct, presumably for the edification of all those interested in this strand of inquiry.   But, we must presume from his review of the sentence-combining literature, such endeavors are discussions in futile search of an audience.

Certainly, Language Arts practitioners owe much to John Mellon, particularly those who would use sentence-combining activity as an instructional method to enhance overall writing quality, to integrate syntactic and rhetorical objectives, and – like in the present study – to integrate the Language Arts with content-area learning. However, Mellon is currently behaving like an anachronism in the context of sentence-combining inquiry. If, as Daiker et al (1985) describe him, Mellon anchors the thematic arc of sentence combining at its historical-experimental pole, then current investigators should be aware that the pot of gold lies somewhere at the arc's other end, toward which our research was an initial step.

CHAPTER 6

FROM THEORY TO PRACTICE

Shaping Behavior

The syntactic treatment described in the preceding chapters clearly focuses on one main outcome, the enhanced expository writing of ninth graders. Now, ninth graders are not unlike other learners. They are not likely to nod affirmatively, yell "Aha," and demonstrate significantly improved performance in response to a clever lesson or two. Especially when those lessons focus on models of cohesive exposition. The veteran practitioner understands that such complex learning outcomes require deliberate, instructional strategies. The veteran practitioner becomes something of an expert in the sequencing and subsuming of smaller instructional units toward the complex outcome. The veteran practitioner understands, from a pragmatic view, Skinner's notion of "shaping" behavior.

At the conceptual core of Skinner's theory of operant conditioning lies the notion that reinforcement can be used to sequentially shape behaviors -- in small, incremental steps -- from comparatively simple precursors of the desired behavior to the more complex, desired behavior. According to Skinner, these incremental steps, or what he called "successive approximations," must be arranged in "some plausible developmental order" (Skinner, 1968). Each step represents an "atom of behavior" or "episode" of instruction that causes the learner to adjust her behavior, moving steadily toward the complex behavior with each successive adjustment. According to Skinner, effective instruction depends on (1) designing each step so that it is easily performed by the learner and (2) positively reinforcing, or rewarding, each incremental change. To demonstrate each incremental change, the learner must actively respond by performing an overt, observable action -- such as combining two or more sentences using specific cues.

The discourse-function sentence-combining approach to writing described in the preceding chapters presumes that the behavior of ninth-grade students can be shaped so that significant gains in measures of their written performance will be eventually observed. Each of the eight units of instruction consists of four incremental steps. In each unit, the first of the four successive approximations elicits single-sentence responses using cued sentence combining as an instructional technique. In one unit, for example, the following problem is presented to elicit an appropriate syntactic solution for coordination (syntactic compounding).

Problem

Food must be supplied to the body.
Food must be supplied in the right amount. (NOT ONLY)
Food must be supplied in the right balance. (BUT ALSO)
The right foods keep the cells working properly. (to)

With very little instruction, the student is able to respond successfully to this stimulus. To produce the solution, the student simply must combine all underlined information into one new sentence. The parenthetical cues must immediately precede the underlined content in each line as each is incorporated in the new sentence. In this case, the appropriate response models a coordination strategy using correlative conjunctions.

Solution

Food must be supplied to the body not only in the right amount but also in the right balance to keep the cells working properly.

This response is reinforced in many ways. The teacher, of course, praises the production of the correct solution. As the practitioner might imagine, the solving of these problems actually becomes fun, a type of large-group word game. Typically, ten to twelve problems like the preceding task are presented to the student in each of the eight instructional units. Each problem models a unique syntactic option for achieving the discourse function targeted in the unit. During this process, the student realizes that he is learning and successfully applying syntactic rules in a manner other than the traditional, infinitely less pleasurable rote method.

The next small step, or successive approximation, toward the production of a cohesive expository composition is the expansion of the response length. Instead of producing a single sentence that models a specific discourse function (like coordination), the student is required to produce a paragraph. With this step, the instructional approach changes from cued to open sentence combining. This change alters the nature of the stimulus. The student is no longer provided cues which signal syntactic options. Thus the cues, as stimuli, are "faded." This means, based on the strength of the conditioned responses elicited during the cued exercises, the student is expected to demonstrate the behavior previously elicited by the cues, even though the cues have been withdrawn.

Like the cued exercises, the open sentence-combing activities require the student to apply appropriate syntactic options to provided text. In the absence of the cues, the stimuli in the open exercises become the juxtaposition of ideas within the paragraph that invite specific rhetorical combinations. At the same time, the structure and content of the expository paragraphs are introduced as stimuli, modeling effective options for the cohesive elaboration of a topic. The following open sentence-combining activity appears in the coordination unit.

Problem

MINERALS ARE NEEDED FOR TISSUE BUILDING.
MINERALS ARE NEEDED FOR   BODY FUNCTIONS.
Calcium helps to form bones and teeth. Magnesium helps to form bones and teeth. Iron helps to form blood cells. Iron helps blood to carry oxygen. The body needs iodine in extremely

small quantity. Iodine is important to the function of the thyroid gland. Sodium is another important mineral. Sodium can be found in table salt. Sodium can be found in butter. Sodium can be found in bacon. Sodium reduces muscle contractions. Sodium aids the transmission of nerve messages.

The format of the problem presents the topic ideas in upper case letters. The balance of the text elaborates on the topic. Both the topic ideas and the other sentences juxtapose content that invites rhetorical (coordination, in this case) and other combinations. The student, who is encouraged to apply any of the coordination options which she learned in the cued exercises, will produce a response resembling the following solution.

Solution

Minerals are needed for tissue building as well as for body functions. Both calcium and magnesium help to form bones and teeth. Iron helps to form blood cells, and it helps the blood to carry oxygen. The body needs iodine, which is important to the function of the thyroid gland, in extremely small quantity. Another important mineral, sodium can be found in table salt, butter, and bacon. Sodium reduces muscle contractions and aids the transmission of nerve messages.

Again, the response is reinforced by teacher praise and by the student's growing satisfaction in his own performance. Students who have historically experienced some difficulty with traditional approaches to grammar instruction and with expository-writing tasks will likely be among the most enthusiastic responders. This affective response -- a feeling of self-esteem associated with, of all things, language arts activity -- is a powerful reinforcer, facilitating the transition to the next of the successive approximations of the targeted, complex behavior.

In the next step, the length of response is expanded further in another open exercise. This time, the student is required to produce *two* paragraphs of cohesive expository text, again in response to content that invites specific rhetorical combinations. In the coordination unit, the underlined and parenthetical cues, faded in the preceding episode, remain absent.

Problem

CARBOHYDRATES ARE USED BY THE BODY AS A SOURCE OF ENERGY. FATS ARE USED BY THE BODY AS A SOURCE OF ENERGY. The body can use any available fats. The body must first use all of its carbohydrate supply. Carbohydrates are available in foods that contain starches. Carbohydrates are available in foods that contain sugars. These foods include pasta. These foods include potatoes. The foods include bread. Approximately two percent of the male body is comprised of carbohydrates. Approximately two percent of the female body is comprised of carbohydrates.

Fats are unlike carbohydrates. Fats can be stored by the body. Foods that are high in fats include dairy products. Foods that are high in fats include cooking oil. Foods that are high in fats include salad dressing. The amount of fat in the male and female bodies is different. The male body contains approximately 18 percent fat. The female body contains about 30 percent fat. The ideal diet contains about 25 percent fat.

The preceding exercise coordinates or links carbohydrates and fats as topic ideas, elaborating first on carbohydrates, then on fats, in the respective paragraphs. In this way, the global structure of the passage springs from the discourse strategy (coordination) that links the topic ideas themselves. Other, obvious invitations to coordinate ideas also exist within each paragraph. Again applying the syntactic options from the cued exercises that result in the coordination of ideas, a student's solution might resemble the following response.

Solution

Carbohydrates and fats are used by the body as a source of energy. Before the body can use any available fats, it must use all of its carbohydrate supply. Carbohydrates are available in foods that contain starches and sugars. These foods include pasta, potatoes, and bread. Approximately two percent of both the male and female body is comprised of carbohydrates.

Unlike carbohydrates, fats can be stored by the body. Foods that are high in fats include dairy products, cooking oils, and salad dressing. And unlike carbohydrates, the amount of fat in male and female bodies is different. The male body contains about 18 percent fat, and the female body about 25 percent fat.

After responses like this are reinforced in the manner previously described, the stimulus for the final successive approximation is introduced in each of the eight instructional units. It is, again and for the final time, an open sentence-combining exercise. This time, the length of the student's response is lengthened to three paragraphs. The three-paragraph open exercise for the coordination unit follows.

Problem

Water supplies no vitamins. Water supplies only small amounts of minerals. WATER IS AN IMPORTANT NUTRIENT FOR THREE REASONS. First, water cools the body. The body produces sweat. Sweat evaporates from the surface of the body. Evaporation is a change from liquid to gas. Evaporation requires heat. When sweat evaporates, the body loses heat. The body's temperature is regulated.

Many chemicals in the body can mix only with water. Fats must be acted upon by enzymes in the digestive system. Proteins must also be acted upon by enzymes. Carbohydrates, too, must be acted upon by enzymes. Vitamins move directly into the digestive system by simply mixing with water. Minerals also move directly into the digestive system by mixing with water. Combining with water, vitamins promote growth. Vitamins also promote tissue repair. Combining with water, minerals build tissue. Minerals also regulate body functions.

Water dissolves wastes. The wastes are carried away from the body tissues. If wastes are not removed from the body, fever can result. Poisoning can result. Even death can result. Among the most poisonous wastes produced by the body is urea. Urea results from the breakdown of body protein. Urea is picked up by the blood. Urea is carried through the kidneys. Approximately one to 2.5 liters of water pass through the kidneys daily. The water dissolves the urea. The water carries the urea away from the kidneys. The water carries the urea into the urinary bladder. The water carries the urea out of the body through the urethra.

Like the one- and two-paragraph open activities, this exercise models not only the sentence structure but also a cohesive passage structure for the targeted discourse function – again, in this case, coordination. Applying the syntactic options that he learned in the cued exercises, the student responds to the open passage by writing a passage resembling the following.

Solution

Although water supplies no vitamins and only small amount of minerals, it is an important nutrient for three reasons. First, water cools the body. The body produces sweat, which evaporates from the surface of the body. Evaporation, a change from liquid to gas, requires heat. When sweat evaporates, the body loses heat, and its temperature is regulated.

Second, many chemicals in the body can mix only with water. Fats, proteins, and carbohydrates must be acted upon by enzymes in the digestive system. However, vitamins and minerals move directly into the digestive system by simply mixing with water. Combining with water, vitamins promote growth and tissue repair, and minerals build tissue and regulate body functions.

Finally, water dissolves wastes, which are carried away from the body tissues. If wastes are not removed by the body, fever, poisoning, even death can result. Among the most poisonous wastes produced by the body is urea, which results from the breakdown of body protein. Urea is picked up by the blood and carried through the kidneys. The one to 2.5 liters of water passing through the kidneys daily dissolve the urea then carry it away from the kidneys, into the urinary bladder, and out of the body through the urethra.

After a similar response is elicited and reinforced, the last of the series of successive approximations is complete. The student is ready to perform the targeted complex behavior, i.e. the composition of an expository essay, *independent of all cues.* To this end, the final writing task in each instructional unit provides no text, thus fading the cues supplied by the content and structure of the one-, two-, and three-paragraph open models. Presumably, the student is ready to independently compose cohesive sentences (microstructure) and networks of sentences within and between paragraphs (macrostructure) as a result of the models presented to her in the cued and open exercises respectively. In the coordination unit, the final writing task requires the student to "(i)dentify and discuss the important features of a balanced diet." Presuming the student has attended to the precursor tasks, he should be able to apply the content knowledge requisite for constructing an informed response, addressing topics that include proteins, carbohydrates, fats, vitamins, minerals, and water. Again, his exposure to models of coordination strategies for both the microstructure and macrostructure of text should enable him to cohesively link ideas. (See the instructional materials for the Coordination and Cause-and-Effect units in the appendix of this chapter for details.)

The Discourse Functions

Coordination, a manner of text organization described in the preceding part of this chapter, is one of many "discourse functions" described by Willis Pitkin (1977b). To understand Pitkin's functions, his notion of "discourse" must first be examined. Pitkin asserts that a single (base) idea like "Ben was hungry" is not discourse. Pitkin observes, however, that discourse results when this idea is combined with another base idea to form a sentence like "Because Ben was hungry, he made a sandwich." Thus, for Pitkin, discourse is a statement that creates a logical relationship between or among base or main ideas.

Now, if that is discourse, what is a discourse function? Again, let's refer to that noteworthy sandwich maker, Ben. When the two base ideas were combined, a relationship emerged between them. The underlying function of the discourse was cause ("Ben was hungry") and effect ("He made a sandwich.") Quite simply, then, "discourse function" should be viewed as the purpose or logic for joining two ideas in coherent discourse. Careful, now. Pitkin's view of discourse might sound familiar to the Language Arts teacher, resembling very traditional notions of rhetoric. However, Pitkin's analysis of discourse logic is not focused on the *structure* of familiar rhetoric modes – narration, description, comparison and contrast, definition, process, analysis, and argumentation. Instead, he was more concerned with the *operations* (like cause-and-effect) that might support any of these modes.

Pitkin identified ten basic functions or strategies of discourse, the eight most important of which were incorporated in our research. All of the functions (like the one in the hungry Ben sentence) consist of the combination of two base ideas. This feature of Pitkin's analysis of discourse -- the combination of an "x" and a "y" proposition -- lends itself quite conveniently to a sentence-combining instructional approach, since the latter joins base clauses to form more syntactically complex ideas. In addition, Pitkin's discourse functions, by their very nature, lend themselves equally well to the formulation of informational or expository ideas, as the examples that follow illustrate. Finally, each of the eight following strategies brings the manipulation of syntax into direct relationship with *broader thinking skills* – prompting, as Suhor (1978) observed, the combination of ideas in a manner dictated by particular logical relationships rather than by narrow, syntactic criteria. As our research suggests, the written performance of ninth graders can be enhanced by an instructional approach that allows the students to exploit the following eight discourse functions, prompting the young writers first to combine and then to cohesively elaborate on "x" and "y" propositions.

1. Coordination

Coordination joins ideas for the purpose of establishing a pair or series of related items. For example, the following cued exercise joins two ideas with parallel prepositional phrases.

Problem

Food must be supplied to the body.
Food must be supplied in the right amount. (NOT ONLY)
Food must be supplied in the right balance. (BUT ALSO)
The right amount and balance of food keep the cells working properly. (TO KEEP)

Solution

Food must be supplied to the body not only in the right amount but also in the right balance to keep the cells working properly.

The syntactic structures presented to the students in the context of Coordination include those containing coordinate conjunctions; adverbs; prepositional phrases; and series of words, phrases, and clauses.

2.   Assertion-Inclusion

Assertion-Inclusion analyzes a particular unit in terms of its subunits. For example, the following cued exercise analyzes starch in terms of its carbohydrate sources.

Problem

Starch is a kind of carbohydrate.
The carbohydrates in corn are starch. (– PARTICULARLY)
The carbohydrates in rice are starch. (,)
The carbohydrates in wheat are starch. (,)
The carbohydrates in potatoes are starch. (, and)
Starch makes up a large part of most people's diets. (--)

Solution

Starch – particularly the carbohydrates in corn, rice, wheat, and potatoes – makes up a large part of most people's diets.

The syntactic structures presented to the students in the context of Assertion-Inclusion include those containing indefinite pronouns and nonrestrictive words, phrases, and clauses. With minimal prompting, students are likely to observe that discourse functions can be embedded. For example, the preceding Assertion-Inclusion exercise contains Coordinated elements (corn, rice, wheat, and potatoes.) The modeling of embedded functions allows the student to appreciate the expressive options fostered by the knowledge of these discourse operations.

3. Assertion-Significance

Assertion-Significance enables the writer to say what he or she finds important about an assertion or to offer an interpretation or a perspective on the assertion. For example, the following cued exercise contains an attached appositive that points to the importance of the heart.

Problem

The organ is a pump.
The organ pumps blood through the circulatory system of complex animals. (that)
The organ is the heart.
The heart is a well designed muscle. (,)
The heart is an efficient muscle. (and)
The muscle sustains life. (that)
The muscle beats more than two billion times. (by beating)
The muscle beats during the normal life span.

Solution

The organ that pumps blood through the circulatory system of complex animals is the heart, a well designed and efficient muscle that sustains life by beating more than two billion times during the normal life span.

The syntactic structures presented to the students in the context of Assertion-Significance include those containing attached and embedded appositives, participial phrases, and dependent clauses; compound verbs; and compound sentences.

4. Cause and Effect

Cause and effect is perhaps the discourse relationship most commonly discussed or modeled by Language Arts teachers. Besides the condition that prompted Ben to make his sandwich, a Cause-and

Effect assertion might discuss a more technical relationship – like the one between hemoglobin and anemia, for example.

Problem

The red blood cells do not contain enough hemoglobin. (If)
The red blood cells do not contain enough iron. (or)
A condition is called anemia. (, then)
Anemia makes a person feel tired. (, which)
Anemia makes a person feel weak. (and)
Anemia is likely to develop. (,)

Solution

If the red blood cells do not contain enough hemoglobin or iron, then a condition called anemia, which makes a person feel tired and weak, is likely to develop.

The syntactic structures presented to the students in the context Cause and Effect are those containing participial and prepositional phrases, adverbial clauses, and compound sentences.

5.   Manner-, Evaluation-, Time-, and Location-Assertion

Pitkin discussed Manner-Assertion, Evaluation-Assertion, Time-Assertion, and Location-Assertion as four discrete functions. Because of their logical and syntactic similarity, the four functions were combined in the present project. In this context, manner, evaluation, time, and location are expressed by adverbial words, phrases, or clauses which elaborate on the main assertion by answering the question "How?" (manner or evaluation), "To what extent?" (manner), "When?" (time), or "Where" (location). The following example models an introductory adverbial clause that details the time or condition of the assertion. Arguably, the introductory adverbial clause in the following example expresses not only time but also causality. Because the targeted complex behavior relies on the broad inclusion of these functions in written performance, students should be encouraged to articulate and apply these interpretive options.

Problem

<u>Food</u> enters our cells. (<u>Once</u>).
<u>Oxygen</u> and other gases <u>enter our cells</u>. (<u>and</u>)
<u>Chemical changes take place</u>. (<u>,</u>)
<u>Carbon dioxide is produced</u>. (<u>, and</u>)
Carbon dioxide is <u>a waste product of the reactions</u>. (<u>as</u>)

Solution

Once food and oxygen enter our cells, chemical changes take place, and carbon dioxide is produced as a waste product of the reactions.

The syntactic structures presented to the students in the context of Manner-, Evaluation-, Time-, and Location-Assertion are those containing adverbial words, phrases and clauses.

6.   Assertion-Intensification and Assertion-Regression

   Like the preceding group of functions, Assertion-Intensification and Assertion-Regression were described by Pitkin as discrete operations. They were, however, combined into one unit of instruction for the present project because of their logical (inverse) relationship.   In Assertion-Intensification, an idea is followed by a second proposition that, in some way, places a stronger or more emphatic focus on the original idea. For example, the base idea in the following exercise makes an assertion about the skeletal system that is limited in scope, making reference only to "important organs."   The attached idea expands that reference from "important organs" to "the entire body," thus emphasizing the role of the skeletal system.

Problem

The skeletal system is <u>a framework</u>. (<u>As</u>)
<u>The skeletal system protects important organs</u>. (<u>,</u>)
The skeletal system <u>supports the entire body</u>. (<u>and, indeed,</u>)

Solution

As a framework, the skeletal system protects important organs and, indeed, supports the entire body.

Inverse to the Assertion-Intensification operation, Assertion-Regression presents an idea then *limits* or, in some way, *tempers* it with an attached idea. For example, the base idea in the following exercise identifies a severe effect of arthritis (immobility). However, the attached idea identifies less severe symptom (pain and swelling).

Problem

Arthritis results in the breakdown of bone.
Arthritis causes an individual to suffer immobility. (, causing)
Arthritis causes an individual to suffer pain. (-- or)
Arthritis causes an individual to suffer swelling. (and)
These occur at the affected joints. (anyway--)

Solution

Arthritis results in the breakdown of bone, causing an individual to suffer immobility -- or pain and swelling anyway -- at the affected joints.

The syntactic structures presented to the students in the context of Assertion-Intensification and Assertion-Regression include nonrestrictive words, phrases, and clauses.

7.   Assertion-Comparison

Assertion-Comparison, a common discourse and rhetorical function, focuses on the similarity between two ideas. The cued sentence-combining exercises invite the student to compare two ideas both literally and figuratively. The following example models a literal comparison between the nervous and all other systems in the human body.

Problem

There are <u>systems in the body</u>. (<u>Like other</u>)
<u>The nervous system</u> is one system. (<u>,</u>)
The nervous system <u>is made of billions of specialized cells</u>.
The cells <u>help to make humans unique among all creatures</u>.
(<u>which</u>)

Solution

Like other systems in the body, the nervous system is made of
billions of specialized cells which help to make humans unique
among all creatures.

Later in the same lesson, the student is invited to use "like" again, but
on this occasion (illustrated below) the comparison is figurative, taking
the form of a simile.

Problem

Neurons are <u>like long, thin wires</u>.
Neurons are arranged <u>in a complex network</u>.
<u>Neurons carry messages</u>. (<u>,</u>)
The messages travel <u>between the brain and all body parts</u>.

Solution

Like long, thin wires in a complex network, neurons carry
messages between the brain and all body parts.

The syntactic structures that model Assertion-Comparison in the cued
exercises include prepositional phrases, adverbial clauses, appositives,
participial phrases, and assertions joined by correlative conjunctions.

8.   Assertion-Contrast

Just as Assertion-Comparison focuses on the similarity between two
ideas, Assertion-Contrast focuses on the differences between them.
The following exercise models this common discourse and rhetorical
function.   It contrasts the absence of guaranteed conception in the

process external fertilization with natural strategies for increasing its likelihood.

Problem

There is no guarantee. (Although)
Egg and sperm will ever meet prior to external fertilization. (that)
Fish and other aquatic animals improve the likelihood of fertilization. (,)
They are giving off thousands of sex cells. (by)
They are gathering in large groups. (and by)

Solution

Although there is no guarantee that egg and sperm will ever meet prior to external fertilization, fish and other aquatic animals improve the likelihood of fertilization by giving off thousands of sex cells and by gathering in large groups.

The syntactic structures that model Assertion-Contrast in the cued exercises include adverbial words, phrases, and clauses; compound sentence parts; and compound sentences.

A Sample Unit

The following pages contain the fourth instructional unit from our research described in the preceding chapters. This unit has been selected because the discourse function that it models, cause and effect, is perhaps the most broadly applied among the respective rhetorical modes. Consistent with the instructional sequence previously discussed in this chapter, the unit consists of one cued exercise, three open exercises, and a final expository writing task.

In addition, the unit is introduced, as each instructional unit is introduced, with a semantic mapping exercise, which outlines the science chapter and content integrated into the Language Arts unit. In each unit of the study described in the preceding chapters, all subjects were initially required to map a specific chapter of their ninth-grade biology text and define new vocabulary. This activity represented an attempt to control knowledge differences between the experimental and control subjects, but it is also just good teaching practice. Practitioners who implement sentence-combining activities, therefore, may opt to include the mapping exercises if students require a review or overview of the science content. If, however, the students are familiar with the topic on which the writing activity is based, such a review might prove superfluous.

CAUSE AND EFFECT

CONTENT SOURCE: KASKEL, A., HUMMER, P.J., & DANIEL, L. (1988). BLOOD. IN *BIOLOGY: AN EVERYDAY EXPERIENCE* (CHAPTER 12). COLUMBUS, OH: MERRILL PUBLISHING.

NAME_____SECTION_____

CUED SENTENCE COMBINING
(ANSWERS BEGIN ON PAGE 112.)

- **Directions**: On each "B" line, combine all underlined "A" ideas into one sentence. The underlined words in parentheses should be used *in front of* the combined ideas. Special instructions might also appear in parentheses.

- **Scoring**: Each of the eleven (11) complete responses is worth nine (9) points. *Partial credit:* Each combination task within a sentence is worth 1.5 points.

1.   *BECAUSE X/Y*

     A.   <u>It is part of the circulatory system.</u> (<u>BECAUSE</u>)
         <u>Blood has two very important functions.</u> (<u>,</u>)
         The blood's functions include <u>delivery.</u> (<u>, namely the</u>)
         Blood delivers <u>nutrients to all parts of the body.</u> (<u>of</u>)
         The blood's functions include <u>pickup.</u> (<u>and the</u>)
         Blood picks up <u>waste products from the cells.</u> (<u>of</u>)

     B. _____
        _____
        _____
        _____
        _____

2.   *X/TO Y (INFINITIVE)*

    A. <u>The blood picks up excess body heat</u>.
        The blood <u>delivers it to the skin</u>. (<u>and</u>)
        The pickup and delivery <u>cool the body</u>. (<u>to</u>)
        The body is cooled <u>during exercise</u>.
        The body is cooled during <u>other periods of exertion</u>.
        (<u>and</u>)

    B. _____

        _____

        _____

        _____

        _____

3.   *WHEN X/Y*

    A. <u>Blood settles in a vessel</u>. (<u>WHEN</u>)
        <u>A test tube</u> is a vessel. (<u>like</u>)
        Blood contains <u>nonliving yellow fluid</u>. (<u>,</u>)
        The nonliving yellow fluid is <u>called plasma</u>.
        Plasma <u>separates from</u> the red blood cells.
        Plasma <u>floats on top of the red blood cells</u>. (<u>and</u>)

    B. _____

        _____

        _____

        _____

        _____

4.   *IF X/THEN Y*

    A. <u>The red blood cells do not contain enough hemoglobin</u>.
        (<u>IF</u>)
        The red blood cells do not contain enough <u>iron</u>. (<u>or</u>)
        <u>A condition</u> is <u>called anemia</u>. (<u>, THEN</u>)
        Anemia <u>makes a person feel tired</u>. (<u>, which</u>)
        Anemia makes a person feel <u>weak</u>. (<u>and</u>)
        Anemia <u>is likely to develop</u>. (<u>,</u>)

B. _____
   _____
   _____
   _____
   _____

5.   *SHOULD X/THEN Y/AND Z*

   A.   The red blood cells can become shaped like half moons.
        (SHOULD)
        They cannot easily pass through the capillaries. (, THEN)
        There is another type of anemia. (, AND)
        It is called sickle-cell anemia.
        Sickle-cell anemia develops under these conditions.

   B. _____
      _____
      _____
      _____
      _____

6.   *AS A RESULT OF X/Y/AND Z*

   A.   Sickle cells have an unusual shape. (AS A RESULT OF
        their)
        The sickle cells clog the capillaries. (,)
        The sickle cells damage body cells. (AND)
        The sickle cells damage organs. (and)
        The sickle cells are depriving them of oxygen. (by)

   B. _____
      _____
      _____
      _____
      _____

7.   *UNLESS X/Y*

    A. <u>The body manufactures a sufficient number of platelets</u>.
        (UNLESS)
        Platelets prevent <u>frequent bruising</u>. (<u>,</u>)
        Platelets prevent <u>hemophilia</u>. (<u>or</u>)
        Hemophilia is <u>a disease in which the blood does not clot</u>.
        (<u>,</u>)
        Either of these conditions <u>will result</u>. (<u>,</u>)

    B. _____
        _____
        _____
        _____
        _____

8.   *SINCE X/Y*

    A. <u>A person's blood will not clot</u>. (<u>SINCE</u>)
        <u>He or she has hemophilia</u>. (<u>if</u>)
        <u>A minor cut can result in the loss of a large amount of
        blood</u>. (<u>,</u>)
        A minor cut can <u>become life threatening</u>. (<u>and</u>)

    B. _____
        _____
        _____
        _____
        _____

9.   *X/Y (PARTICIPIAL PHRASE)*

    A. The human body cannot tolerate <u>the mixture of type A and
        type B blood in the circulatory system</u>.
        This mixture <u>is a deadly combination</u>.
        This mixture forms <u>large clumps of blood cells</u>.
        (<u>, FORMING</u>)
        These clumps <u>block vessels in the heart</u>. (<u>which</u>)
        These clumps block vessels in the <u>brain</u>. (<u>,</u>)
        These clumps block vessels in the <u>lungs</u>. (<u>, and</u>)

B. _____
   _____
   _____
   _____
   _____

10.   *X/Y (ADJECTIVE CLAUSE)*

A.   The human body cannot tolerate the mixture of type A
     and type B blood in the circulatory system.
     The mixture is a deadly combination.
     The mixture joins the protein on the red blood cell. (that)
     The mixture joins the protein in the plasma. (with)
     The mixture plugs up the blood vessels. (and)

B. _____
   _____
   _____
   _____
   _____

11.   *X:Y (COMPOUND INDEPENDENT CLAUSES)*

A.   The immune system defends the body from disease.
     It is made up of cells. (: it)
     It is made up of tissues. (and)
     The cells and tissues identify and destroy viruses. (that)
     The cells and tissues identify and destroy bacteria. (and)

B. _____
   _____
   _____
   _____
   _____

x/y

CAUSE AND EFFECT

CONTENT SOURCE: KASKEL, A., HUMMER, P.J., & DANIEL, L. (1988). BLOOD. IN *BIOLOGY: AN EVERYDAY EXPERIENCE* (CHAPTER 12). COLUMBUS, OH: MERRILL PUBLISHING.

NAME_____SECTION_____

OPEN SENTENCE COMBINING
(MODEL RESPONSES BEGIN ON PAGE 113.)

- **Directions**: Study each of the following passages, and then rewrite it in a better way. The topic ideas of each passage appear in upper-case letters. As you rewrite, first combine the topic ideas into a cause-and-effect relationship. Use the sentence patterns that you practiced in the cued exercises. Then, rewrite the rest of the sentences to create a better, more mature style. You may combine sentences, change the order of words, and omit words that are repeated too many times. Be careful, however, not to leave out any information.

- **Scoring**: Each passage will receive one of the following grades: 4=excellent, 3=good, 2=acceptable, 1=unacceptable.

1. *AIDS*

ACQUIRED IMMUNE DEFICIENCY SYNDROME IS A DISEASE. THE DISEASE ATTACKS THE HUMAN SYSTEM. THE DISEASE DESTROYS THE IMMUNE SYSTEM. THE DISEASE MAKES A PERSON VERY SUSCEPTIBLE TO OTHER DISEASES. AIDS is caused by a virus. The virus can reproduce only inside a certain type of white blood cell. The white blood cell is needed by the immune system. This type of white blood cell decreases in number. The body cannot fight other diseases. The number of white blood cells drops to zero. The other diseases eventually cause death. The AIDS virus can be passed from one person to another during sexual contact. The AIDS virus can be passed from a woman to her unborn child during pregnancy. The AIDS virus can be passed form one intravenous drug user to another. The intravenous drug users share the same needle. The AIDS virus can be passed from donor to recipient during a blood transfusion.

_____
_____
_____
_____
_____
_____
_____
_____
_____
_____
_____
_____
_____
_____

2.   *White Blood Cells and the Immune System*

CERTAIN WHITE BLOOD CELLS MAKE SPECIAL CHEMICALS. THESE CHEMICALS ARE CALLED ANTIBODIES. ANTIBODIES DESTROY BACTERIA CELLS. Antibodies can be connected to the white cell membrane. Antibodies can also be released into the blood plasma. Antibodies attack foreign substances. These substances are called antigens. These substances invade the body. These substances cause disease. Antibody attaches itself to an antigen. The antigen can be destroyed in different ways. First, one antibody can tear apart the antigen's membrane. This kills the foreign cell quickly. Second, one antibody can attach itself to an antigen. The antibody can wait for assistance from other antibodies. The antibodies eventually smother the virus or bacteria.

The virus or bacterium cell is destroyed. Then the immune system behaves in a remarkable way. The immune system makes many new white blood cells. Each new white blood cell is made with the shape of the antibody. The antibody just destroyed the antigen. The white blood cells will reproduce the same type of antibody in the bloodstream forever. This will prevent future disease. The disease is caused by the same type of bacterium. The bacterium might invade the body ten years later. The white blood cells with the special antibodies will attack the bacterium very quickly. The person might not even realize that he or she was invaded by the antigen.

_____
_____
_____
_____
_____
_____
_____
_____
_____
_____
_____
_____
_____
_____
_____
_____
_____
_____
_____

3.   *The Coagulation (Clotting) of Blood*

THE COAGULATION OF BLOOD IS A COMPLEX PROCESS. THE PROCESS IS CONTROLLED BY ENZYMES. THE PROCESS IS CONTROLLED BY PHYSICAL FACTORS. A blood vessel is cut or punctured. Blood loses its fluid properties. Blood becomes a semisolid mass. In the process, the enzyme thrombin produces fibrin. Fibrin is a protein. Fibrin forms a meshwork. The meshwork traps blood cells. The meshwork traps plasma. The meshwork eventually creates the clot.

Blood does not normally clot in uncut or unpunctured vessels. Anticoagulants in the blood prevent clotting. Heparin acts as a natural anticoagulant. Heparin interferes with thrombin's ability to produce fibrin. The body produces only small amounts of heparin. Doctors sometimes prescribe doses of heparin to patients. The heparin reduces the danger of clot formation inside the blood vessels.

Physical factors affect blood coagulation. The most common of these factors are temperature, the condition of the tissue, and the presence of water. Blood is carefully refrigerated. Blood will remain fluid for longer periods of time. Platelets contact rough surfaces like cut tissue. The platelets are rapidly destroyed. The formation of a clot is stimulated. Blood makes contact with a surface wetted by water. The clotting process is hastened. However, blood is collected in a tube. The tube is coated with a layer of wax or paraffin. The clotting process will be greatly prolonged.

CAUSE AND EFFECT

CONTENT SOURCE: KASKEL, A., HUMMER, P.J., & DANIEL, L. (1988). BLOOD. IN *BIOLOGY: AN EVERYDAY EXPERIENCE* (CHAPTER 12). COLUMBUS, OH: MERRILL PUBLISHING.

NAME_____SECTION_____

EXPOSITORY WRITING

- **Directions**: Think about the information concerning blood in Chapter 12 of your biology text. You may refer to the chapter map in your notes to help you remember the subtopics and important details. Use this information in response to the following task.

  Your response must be at least ten (10) sentences organized as one or more paragraphs. As you write the sentences, think of the cause-and-effect structures that were modeled in the cued sentence-combining exercises. Think also about the structure of the one- two- and three-paragraph passages in the open sentence combining exercises.

- **Scoring**: Each passage will receive one of the following grades: 4=excellent, 3=good, 2=acceptable, 1=unaccept-ble.

WRITING TASK: EXPLAIN HOW BLOOD SUPPORTS HUMAN LIFE.

x/y

CAUSE AND EFFECT

CONTENT SOURCE: KASKEL, A., HUMMER, P.J., & DANIEL, L. (1988).   BLOOD.   IN *BIOLOGY: AN EVERYDAY EXPERIENCE* (CHAPTER 12).   COLUMBUS, OH: MERRILL PUBLISHING.

- **CUED RESPONSES**

1.   Because it is part of the circulatory system, blood has two very important functions, namely the delivery of nutrients to all parts of the body and the pickup of waste products from the cells.

2.   The blood picks up excess body heat and delivers it to the skin to cool the body during exercise and other periods of exertion.

3.   When blood settles in a vessel like a test tube, nonliving yellow fluid called plasma separates from and floats on top of the red blood cells.

4.   If the red blood cells do not contain enough hemoglobin or iron, then a condition called anemia, which makes a person feel tired and weak, is likely to develop.

5.   Should the red blood cells become shaped like half moons, then they cannot easily pass through the capillaries, and another type of anemia called sickle-cell anemia occurs.

6.   As a result of their unusual shape, the sickle cells clog the capillaries and damage body cells and organs by depriving them of oxygen.

7.   Unless the body manufactures a sufficient number of platelets, frequent bruising or hemophilia, a disease in which the blood does not clot, will result.

8.   Since a person's blood will not clot if he or she has hemophilia, a minor cut can result in the loss of a large amount of blood and become life threatening.

9.   The mixture of type A and type B blood in the circulatory system is a deadly combination, forming large clumps of red blood cells which block vessels in the heart, brain, and lungs.

10. The mixture of type A and type B blood in the circulatory system is a deadly combination, that joins the protein on the red blood cell with the protein in the plasma and plugs up the blood vessels..

11. The immune system defends the body from disease: it is made up of cells and tissues that identify and destroy viruses and bacteria.

- **MODEL OPEN RESPONSES**

AIDS.

Acquired Immune Deficiency Syndrome is a disease that attacks and destroys the immune system, making a person very susceptible to other diseases. AIDS is caused by a virus which can reproduce only inside a certain type of white blood cell needed by the immune system. When this type of white blood cell decreases, the body cannot fight other diseases. When the number of white blood cells drops to zero, the other diseases eventually cause death. The AIDS virus can be passed from one person to another during sexual contact, from a woman to her unborn child during pregnancy, from one intravenous drug user to another if they share a needle, or from donor to recipient during a blood transfusion.

WHITE BLOOD CELLS AND THE IMMUNE SYSTEM.

Certain white blood cells make special chemicals called antibodies that destroy both bacteria and virus cells. Antibodies can be either connected to the white-cell membrane or released into the blood plasma. Antibodies attack foreign substances called antigens which invade the body and cause disease. When an antibody attaches itself to an antigen, the antigen can be destroyed in different ways. First, an antibody can tear apart the antigen's membrane, killing the foreign cell quickly, Second, one antibody can attach itself to an antigen and wait for assistance from other antibodies, who eventually smother the virus or bacterium.

After the virus or bacterium cell is destroyed, the immune system behaves in a remarkable way. The immune system makes many new white blood cells, each of which is made with the shape of the antibody that just destroyed the antigen. The white blood cells will reproduce the same type of antibody in the bloodstream forever, preventing future disease caused by the same bacteria. If that bacterium invades the body ten years later, the white blood cells with the special antibodies will attack it so quickly that the person might not even realize that he or she was invaded by the antigen

- *THE COAGULATION (CLOTTING) OF THE BLOOD.*

The coagulation of blood is a complex process controlled by both enzymes and physical factors. After a blood vessel is cut or punctured, blood loses its fluid properties and becomes a semisolid mass. In the process, the enzyme thrombin produces the protein fibrin. Fibrin forms a meshwork that traps blood cells and plasma, eventually creating the clot.

Blood does not normally clot in uncut or unpunctured vessels because anticoagulants in the blood prevent clotting. Heparin, which acts as a natural anticoagulant, interferes with thrombin's ability to produce fibrin. Because the body produces only small amounts of heparin, doctors sometimes prescribe doses of it to patients to reduce the danger of clot formation inside the blood vessels.

The most common physical factors that affect blood coagulation are temperature, the condition of the tissue, and the presence of water. When blood is carefully refrigerated, it will remain fluid for longer periods of time. If platelets contact rough surfaces like cut tissue, they are rapidly destroyed, and the formation of a clot is stimulated. If blood makes contact with a surface wetted by water, then the clotting process is hastened. However, should blood be collected in a tube that is coated with a layer of wax or paraffin, then the clotting process is greatly prolonged.

APPENDIX

**SHAWSHEEN VALLEY TECHNICAL HIGH SCHOOL
ENGLISH AND READING DEPARTMENT**

**SHAWSHEEN WRITING TEST, FORM B
COMPARISON AND CONTRAST**

TEST DATE_____

STUDENT INFORMATION

- NAME (LAST, FIRST)_____
- SEPTEMBER GRADE ____9____10____11____12
- DATE OF BIRTH____MONTH____DAY____YEAR

- TOWN _____BEDFORD
  _____BILLERICA
  _____BURLINGTON
  _____TEWKSBURY
  _____WILMINGTON
  _____OTHER (SPECIFY)_____

- SCHOOL_____MARSHALL MIDDLE
  _____LOCKE MIDDLE
  _____WYNN MIDDLE
  _____NORTH INTERMEDIATE
  _____WEST INTERMEDIATE
  _____GLENN JUNIOR HIGH
  _____MARSHALL SIMONDS MIDDLE
  _____OTHER (SPECIFY)_____

ABOUT THIS TEST: YOU WILL WRITE A BRIEF ESSAY ON A TOPIC THAT IS VERY FAMILIAR TO YOU. NO ONE FAILS THIS TEST. TWO ENGLISH TEACHERS WILL READ YOUR ESSAY (1) TO IDENTIFY YOUR STRENGTHS AND WEAKNESSES AS A WRITER AND (2) TO HELP DETERMINE YOUR PLACMENT IN AN ENGLISH COURSE.

Step 1, Read the topic...

> **Read this silently as the teacher reads aloud.**
>
> Some teachers are very effective. Their students seem to enjoy learning and coming to class. Unfortunately, other teachers are ineffective. Their students simply do not seem to enjoy coming to class.
>
> A regional educational committee is currently asking local students to give their opinions about effective and ineffective teaching. The committee will present special awards to the most effective teachers in the region. In addition, the committee will sponsor workshops to improve the quality of ineffective teaching in these towns.
>
> What do you think? What types of teachers or teaching styles should receive special awards? What types of teachers or teaching styles need improvement?
>
> Your assignment is to write an essay comparing effective and ineffective teachers and their styles of teaching.
>
> *PLEASE DO NOT IDENTIFY ANY SPECIFIC TEACHERS, SCHOOLS, OR TOWNS.*

Step 2, Outline your ideas (optional)...

> **Use these lines to organize your main ideas and/or important details.**

Step 3, Write, revise, and edit a rough draft...

Use these lines to write a rough draft. After you finish the draft, revise (change) any words or groups of words. Edit (correct) your spelling, capitalization, and punctuation. Neatness is not important. If you need more space, ask the teacher for a piece of composition paper.

Step 4, Write your final copy...

Use these lines to write the final copy of your essay. Write clear and complete sentences in a well organized paragraph or in well organized paragraphs.   Pay attention to grammar, spelling, capitalization, and punctuation. Be as neat as possible. Again, if you need more space, ask the teacher for a piece of composition paper.

x/y

Content source: Kaskel, A., Hummer, P., & Daniel, L. (1988). Nutrition. In *Biology: An Everyday Experience* (Chapter 9). New York: Merrill Publishing.

Name_____ Section_____

Directions: In the following map of Chapter 9, fill-in the appropriate topic (center circle), subtopics (numbered circle headings), and details (inside each circle, below heading). You may refer to the list of terms that accompany the map.

Scoring: The forty (40) items are worth 2.5 points each.

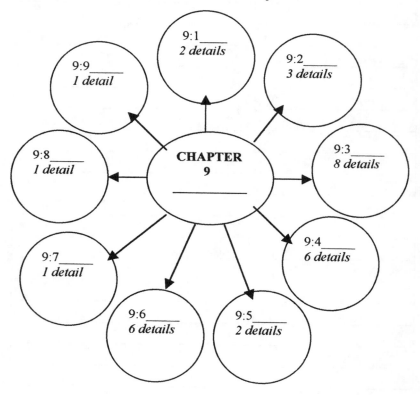

x/y

Content source: Kaskel, A., Hummer, P., & Daniel, L. (1988).
Nutrition. In *Biology: An Everyday Experience* (Chapter 9). New
York: Merrill Publishing.

CHAPTER 9, LIST OF TERMS

Directions: Use the following terms as the topic, subtopics, and details
to complete the Chapter 9 map. Terms that appear more than once on
the map also appear more than once in this alphabetical list.

1. Adult intake
2. Ascorbic acid
3. Balanced diet
4. Calciferol
5. Calcium
6. Calorie
7. Calorie of content of food given equal massed
8. Calorie content of food
9. Carbohydrates
10. Composition of human body
11. Energy in food
12. Factors contributing to weight gain
13. Fats
14. Fat-carbohydrate group
15. Food
16. Fruit-vegetable group
17. Grain group
18. Iodine
19. Iron
20. Magnesium
21. Meat group
22. Milk group
23. Minerals
24. Minerals
25. Niacin
26. Nutrients
27. Nutrition
28. Nutrition
29. Proteins
30. Protein, fat, carbohydrate
31. RDA
32. Retinol
33. Riboflavin
34. Sodium
35. Supplying nutrients to the body
36. Thiamine
37. Using calories
38. Vitamins
39. Vitamins
40. Water

APPENDIX TABLE.   CONTROL GROUP: SEQUENCE OF SYNTAX TOPICS,   IN-CLASS   ACTIVITIES,   HOMEWORK   ASSIGNMENTS, AND TESTS

WK	TOPIC	IN-CLASS ACTIVITY	HOMEWORK	TESTS
1	Nouns	The Noun, P 3-4, Ex 1 Common, Proper P 4-5, Ex 2	Capitalization P 455-6 Ex B	Capital Letters P 103.
		Capitalization P 441-458 Ex C, p 456		
	Pronouns	The Pronoun P 6-7	Pronouns Ex 5, p 10	Pronouns P 3
		Types of Pronoun P 8-10, Ex 4		
2	Pronouns	Case Forms P 180-1, Ex 1	Nominative, Objective Case P 186-8 Ex A	Prnoun Subject P 77
		Nominative Case P 180-4, Ex 3-5		Predicate Nominatives P 78
		Objective Case P 184-6, Ex 6-8		
	Prepositional Phrases	Preposition P 29-30, Ex 21	Nominative, Objective Case P 190, Ex B	Direct, Indirect Objects P 79
		Objects P 188-9 Ex 9-10		Objects P 80
3	Verbs	The Verb P 15-16	Action Verb P 17, Ex 10	Action Verbs Linking Verbs P 6
		The Action Verb P 16-17, Ex 9	Linking Verb P 20, Ex 13	
		The Linking Verb P 17-19, Ex 11		Helping Verbs P 11
		Verb Phrases P 20-22, Ex 14		
4	Pronoun Agreement	Antecedent Agreement P 147-51 Ex 10, 11	Antecedent Agreement P 151-2, Ex F	Antecedent Agreement P 62

WK	TOPIC	IN-CLASS ACTIVITY	HOMEWORK	TESTS
4	Subject-Verb Agreement	Agreement P 129-30, Ex 1	Subject-Verb Agreement P 133 Ex 4	Subject-Verb Agreement P 55, 57
		Subj-Verb Agreement P 130-37 Ex 2, 3, 5		
		Compound Subject P 137-40 Ex 6, Rev C		
5	Modifiers	The Adjective P10-15, Ex 6	The Adjective P14-15, Ex A	Adjectives P 4, Even
		The Adverb P 22-28 Ex 15-19	The Adverb P27-8, Ex 20	Adverbs P 14, Odd
		Correct Usage P 202-210 Ex 1,2, A, 7	Correct Usage P 209-210 Review Ex B	Regular Comparison P 84, Even
				Irregular Comparison P 86, Odd
6	Verbals, Verbal Phrases	The Participle P 88-91, Ex 6	The Participial Phrase Teacher's Ed P 28	Participial Phrases P 29, Even
		The Participial Phrase P 91-2, Ex 3		Gerund Phrases P 31, Odd
		The Gerund P 93-9, Ex 9	The Gerund Teacher's Ed P 30	
		The Infinitive P 98-9, Ex 11	The Infinitive Phrase Teacher's Ed P 33	Infinitives, Infinitive Phrases P 34, Even
		The Infinitive Teacher's Ed P 32		
		Misplaced Modifiers P 214-16 Ex 11	Dangling and Misplaced Modifiers P 214-16 Ex 11, Odd	Dangling Modifiers P 87, Odd
				Misplaced Modifiers P 89
7	Appositives	Appositives P 102-5 Ex 14	Appositve Phrse Teacher's Ed P 36	Appositives P 35, Odd

WK	TOPIC	IN-CLASS ACTIVITY	HOMEWORK	TESTS
7	Selected Punctuation	Comma, series P 463-5, Ex 3	Comma, series Teacher's Ed P 190	Commas, Interrupters P 198, Even
		Dashes P 532-3, Ex 3	Comma, compound sentence Teacher's Ed P 192	Comma, compound sentence P 193, Odd
		Parentheses P 533-4, Ex 4		Semicolons P 201, Even
		Joining independent clauses P 467-70, Ex 6 P 489-92, Ex 1	Semicolons Teacher's Ed P 200	
8	Dependent, Independent Clauses	Dependent, Independent Clauses P 106-8, Ex 1	Dependent, Independent Clauses Teacher's Ed P 39	Adjectve Clause P 42, Even
		Adjective Clause P 109-13 Ex 2, 3	Adjectve Clause Teacher's Ed P 40	Who, Whom P 82, Odd
		Who and Whom P 190-195 Ex 11, 12	Who and Whom Teacher's Ed P 81	Subordinating Conjunctions P 44, 1-15
		Adverb Clause P 113-117 Ex 6	Adverb Clause Teacher's Ed P 43	Noun Clauses P 46, 1-15
		Noun Clause P 115-17 Ex 8	Noun Clause Teacher's Ed P 45	

All activities and homework (except where noted) from J.E. Warriner, M.E. Whitten, & F. Griffith. (1977). *Warriner's English grammar and composition, Third Course.* New York: Harcourt, Brace, & Jovanovich. All tests (except where noted) from J.E. Warriner, M.E. Whitten, & F. Griffith. (1988). *Warriner's English grammar and composition, Third Course.* Teacher's Edition, Part I. Reteaching/Enrichment Worksheets. New York: Harcourt, Brace, & Jovanovich.

REFERENCES

Ackerman, B. (1986). Referential and causal coherence in the story comprehension of children and adults. *Journal of Experimental Child Psychology, 41,* 336-366.

Ausubel, D.P. (1960). The use of advance organizers in the learning of and retention of meaningful verbal material. *Journal of Educational Psychology, 51,* 267-272.

Anderson, J. (1985). *Cognitive psychology and its implications.* New York: WH Freeman.

Ashcraft, M. (1994). *Human memory and cognition.* New York: Harper Collins.

Belanger, J.F. (1978). Calculating the syntactic density score: A mathematical problem. *Research in the Teaching of English: 12,* 149-153.

Bond, C.A. (1972). A new approach to freshman composition: A trial of the Christensen method. *College English, 33,* 623-627.

Braddock, R., Lloyd-Jones, R., & Schoer, L. (1963). *Research in written composition.* Champaign, Ill: National Council of the Teachers of English, Eric Document 003374.

Brereton, J. (1979). How reliable are T-units? Paper presented at the conference on College Composition and Communication.

Broadhead, G.J., & Berlin, J.A. (1981). Twelve steps to using generative sentences and sentence combining in the composition classroom. *College Composition and Communication, 32(3),* 295-307.

Callaghan, T.F. (1997). The effects of sentence-combining exercises on the syntactic maturity, quality of writing, reading ability, and attitudes of ninth-grade students. Unpublished doctoral dissertation. State University of New York at Buffalo.

Campbell, D., & Fisk, D. (1959). Convergent and discriminant validity by the multitrait-multimethod matrix. *Psychological Bulletin, 54,* 81-105.

Campbell, D.T., & Stanley, J.C. (1963). Experimental and quasi-experimental designs for research. Chicago: Rand McNally & Company.

Carifio, J. (1993). Needed: A standard model of information processing and learning. ERIC Document TM019683.

Center for Labor Market Studies at Northeastern University. (1993). Social and economic change in the Shawsheen Valley communities: Findings from the 1980 and 1990 censuses. A report prepared for the Massachusetts Occupational Information Coordinating Committee and the Division of Occupational Education, Massachusetts Department of Education.

Chomsky, N. (1985). *Knowledge of language: Its nature, origin, and use.* New York: Praeger.

Christensen, F. (1963). A generative rhetoric of the sentence. *College Composition and Communication, 16:* 114-146.

_____. (1965). A generative rhetoric of the paragraph. *College Composition and Communication, 16:* 144-146.

_____. (1967). *Notes toward a new rhetoric: Six essays for teachers.* New York: Harper and Row.

_____. (1968). *The Christensen rhetoric program.* New York: Harper and Row.

Combs, W.E. (1975). Some further effects and implications of sentence-combining exercises for the secondary language-arts curriculum. Unpublished doctoral dissertation, University of Minnesota.

Cooper, C.R. (1977). Holistic evaluation of writing. In C.R. Cooper, & L. Odell (Eds.) *Evaluating writing: Describing, measuring, judging.* (pp. 3-31). Urbana, Ill: National Council of the Teachers of English.

Crowhurst, M. (1977). The effects of intended audience and mode of discourse on the syntactic complexity of student writing in grades 6 and 10. Unpublished doctoral dissertation, University of Minnesota.

_____. (1980). Syntactic complexity and teachers' quality ratings of narration and arguments. *Research in the Teaching of Writing, 14,* 223-231.

Crowhurst, M., & Piche, G.L. (1979). Audience and mode of discourse effects on syntactic complexity in writing at two grade levels. *Research in the Teaching of English, 13,* 101-109.

Dagostino, L., & Carifio, J. (1994). *Evaluative reading and literacy: A cognitive view.* Boston: Allyn and Bacon.

D'Angelo, F.J. (1974). A generative rhetoric of the essay. *College Composition and Communication, 25,* 388-396.

Davis, F.B. (1972). Psychometric research on comprehension in reading. *Reading Research Quarterly, 7,* 628-678.

Diederich, P.B. (1966). How to measure growth in writing ability. *English Journal, 55,* 435-449.

Diederich, P.B., French, J.W., & Carlton, S.T. (1961). Factors in judgments of writing ability. *Research Bulletin 61-15.* Princeton, NJ: Educational Testing Service.

Elley, W.B., Barham, I.H., Lamb, H., & Wyllie, M. (1976). The role of grammar in a secondary school English curriculum. *Research in Teaching English, 10,* 5-21. ERIC Document 112410.

Faigley, L. (1979). The influence of generative rhetoric on the syntactic maturity and writing effectiveness of college freshmen. *Research in the Teaching of English, 13(3),* 197-206.

_____. (1985). Performative assessment of writing skills. In D. Daiker, A. Kerek, & M. Morenberg, M. (Eds.) *Sentence combining: A rhetorical perspective.* (pp. 175-186). Carbondale, Ill: Southern Illinois University Press: 175-186.

Franklin, S. (1995). *Artificial minds.* Cambridge, MA: MIT Press.

Frederiksen, C.H. (1987). Knowledge representation and discourse: Producing and communicating meaning. Paper presented at the Conference on College Composition and Communication. National Council of Teachers of English. ERIC Document 281154.

Goodman, K.S. (1970). Behind the eye: What's happening in reading. In *Reading: processes and program.* Urbana: Ill: National Council of Teachers of English.

Grady, M.A. (1971). A conceptual rhetoric of the composition. *College Composition and Communication, 22,* 348-354.

Graves, M.F. (1984). Selecting vocabulary to teach in the intermediate and secondary grades. In J. Flood (Ed.) *Promoting reading comprehension.* Newark, DE: International Reading Association.

Green, E.A. (1972). An experimental study of sentence combining to improve written syntactic fluency in fifth-grade children. Unpublished doctoral dissertation, Northern Illinois University.

Hazen, C.L. (1972). The relative effectiveness of two methodologies in the development of composition skills in college freshman English. An unpublished doctoral dissertation, North Texas State University.

Henning, K.R. (1980). Composition writing and the function of language. Unpublished doctoral dissertation, State University of New York at Buffalo.

Hilfman, T. (1970). Can second-grade children write more complex sentences? *Elementary English, 47,* 209-214.

Hillocks, G. (1986). *Research on written compositions: New directions for teaching.* Urbana, Ill: National Conference on Research in English.

Hunt, K.W. (1965). *Grammatic structures written at three grade levels.* NCTE Research Report No. 3. Champaign, Ill: National Council of the Teachers of English.

Hunt, K.W., & O'Donnell, R.C. (1970). *An elementary school curriculum to develop better writing skills.* Cooperative research project No. 8-0903. Florida State University. ERIC Document 050108

Johnson, S.T. (1969). Some tentative strictures on generative rhetoric. *College English, 31,* 155-165.

Jones, M.A.C. (1980). Sentence combining: Measuring the rate of syntactic growth in freshman composition. ERIC Document 208391.

Jurgens, J.M., & Griffin, W.J. (1970). Relationships between overall quality and seven language features in compositions written in grades seven, nine, and eleven. Nashville: George Peabody College for Teachers. ERIC Document 046932.

Kanellas, R.J., Mello, M., & Poulten, G. (1991). *Shawsheen Writing Test.* Billerica, MA: Shawsheen Technical High School.

Karlsen, B., Gardner, E.F., & Madden, R. (1984). *Stanford Diagnostic Reading Test,* blue level, form G. Dallas: Harcourt, Brace, & Jovanovich.

Kerek, A., Daiker, D., & Morenberg, M. (1980). Sentence combining and college composition. *Perceptual and Motor Skills, 51,* 1059-1157.

Kerlinger, F.N. (1986). *Foundations of behavioral research.* (3'rd Ed.). New York: Holt, Rinehart, & Winston.

LaBerge, D., & Samuels, S.J. (1976). Toward a theory of automatic information processing in reading. In H. Singer & R.B. Ruddell (Eds.), *Theoretical models and processes of reading* (2'nd Ed.). Newark, DE: International Reading Association.

Landwehr, J. (1980). Generative rhetoric sentence combining: A new approach to expository writing. Paper presented to the Annual Meeting of the Conference of College Composition and Communication. ERIC Document 185582.

Maimon, E.P., & Nodine, B.F. (1978). Measuring syntactic growth: Errors and expectations in sentence-combining practice with college freshmen. *Research in the Teaching of English, 12,* 233-244.

Martinez San-Jose, C.P. (1973). See San-Jose, C. (1972).

Mellon, J.C. (1969). *Transformational sentence combining: A method for enhancing the development of syntactic fluency in English composition.* Urbana, Ill: National Council of Teachers of English.

_____ (1979). Issues in the theory and practice of sentence combining: A twenty-year perspective. In D.A. Daiker, A. Kerek, & M. Morenberg (Eds.), *Sentence combining and the teaching of writing* (pps. 1-38). Akron, OH: L&S Books, University of Akron.

_____ (1985). The role of the elaborated dominant nominalin the measurement of syntactic and conceptual fluencies in expository writing. In D. Daiker, A. Kerek, &M. Morenberg (Eds.), *Sentence combining: A rhetorical perspective*. Carbondale, Ill: Southern Illinois University Press.

Miller, B.D., & Ney, J.W. (1968). The effect of systematic oral exercises on the writing of fourth-grade students. *Research in the Teaching of English, 2,* 44-61.

Mulder, J.E.M., Braun, C., & Holliday, W.G. (1978). The effects of sentence-combining practice on the linguistic maturity level of adult students. *Adult Education, 28,* 11-20.

Neisser, U. (1967). *Cognitive psychology*. New York: Appleton-Century-Crofts.

Ney, J.W. (1976). The hazards of the course: Sentence combining in freshman English. *The English Record, 27,* 70-77.

Nietzke, D.A. (1972). The influence of composition assignment upon grammatical structure. Unpublished doctoral dissertation, University of Illinois at Urban-Champaign.

Nold, E.W., & Freedman, S.W. (1977). An analysis of readers' responses to essays. *Research in the Teaching of English, 11,* 164-174.

O'Donnell, R.C., Griffin, W.J., & Norris, R.C. (1967). Syntax of kindergarten and elementary school children: A transformational analysis. Urbana, Ill: National Council of Teachers of English.

Ofsa, W.J. (1974). An experiment in using research in composition in the training of teachers of English. Unpublished doctoral dissertation, University of Illinois, Urbana-Champagne.

O'Hare, F. (1971). The effect of sentence-combining practice not dependent on formal knowledge of a grammar on the writing of seventh graders. Unpublished doctoral dissertation, Florida State University.

Pederson, E.L. (1977). Improving syntactic and semantic fluency in the writing of language-arts students through extended practice in sentence combining. Unpublished doctoral dissertation, University of Minnesota.

Perron, J.D. (1974). An exploratory approach to extending the syntactic development of fourth-grade students through the use of sentence-combining methods. Unpublished doctoral dissertation, University of Minnesota.

_____. (1976). Beginning writing: It's all in the mind. *Language Arts, 53,* 652-657.

Pitkin, W. (1977a). Hierarchies and the discourse hierarchy. *College English, 38,* 649-659.

_____. (1977b). X/Y: Some basic strategies of discourse hierarchy. *College English, 38,* 661-672.

_____. (1978). Hierarchal base combining. Unpublished paper.

Rice, P.H. (1983). A study of the effectiveness of sentence combining in increasing the syntactic maturity of students writing at grades 7 through 11. Unpublished doctoral dissertation, University of Cincinnati.

Rose, S.K. (1983). Down from the haymow: One hundred years of sentence combining. *College English, 45,* 483-491.

Ruddell, R., & Speaker, R.B. (1985). The interactive reading process: A model. In H. Singer & R. Ruddell (Eds.), *Theoretical models and processes of reading.* Newark, DE: International Reading Association: 751-793.

San Jose, C. (1972). Grammatic structures in four modes of writing at the fourth-grade level. Unpublished doctoral dissertation, Syracuse University.

_____. (1978). Letter. *Research in the teaching of English, 12:* 91-92.

Schuster, E.H. (1977). Using sentence combining to teach writing to inner-city students. Paper presented to the National Council of Teachers of English conference. ERIC Document 150614.

Stewart, M.F. (1978). Freshman sentence combining: A Canadian project. *Research in the Teaching of English, 12,* 257-268.

Stewart, M.F., & Lehman, H.L. (1979). Syntactic maturity, mechanics of writing, and teachers' quality ratings. *Research in the Teaching of English, 13,* 207-215.

Stotsky, S. (1975). Sentence combining as a curricular activity: Its effects on written language development and reading comprehension. *Research in the Teaching of English, 9,* 30-71.

Straw, S.B. (1978). The effect of sentence combining and sentence reduction instruction on measures of syntactic fluency, reading comprehension, and listening comprehension in fourth-grade students. Unpublished doctoral dissertation, University of Minnesota.

Strong, W. (1973). *Sentence combining: A composing book.* New York: Random House.

Suhor, C. (1978). Sentence manipulation and cognitive operations. Paper presented to the Boston University Conference on Language Development. ERIC Document 166692.

Sullivan, M.A. (1977). The effects of sentence combining exercises on syntactic maturity, quality of writing, reading ability, and attitudes of students in grade eleven. Unpublished doctoral dissertation, State University of New York at Buffalo.

Swan, M.B. (1977). The effects of instruction in transformational sentence combining on the syntactic complexity and quality of college-level writing. Unpublished doctoral dissertation, Boston University.

Thibodeau, A.E. (1964). Improving composition writing with grammar and organization exercises utilizing differentiated group patterns. Unpublished doctoral dissertation, University of Wisconsin.

Tibbetts, A.M. (1970). On the practical uses of a grammatical system: A note on Christensen and Johnson. *College English, 31,* 870-878.

van Dijk, T.A., & Kintsch, W. (1983). *Strategies of discourse comprehension.* New York: Academic Press.

Vitale, M.R., King,F.J., Shontz, D.W., & Huntley, G.M. (1971). Effects of sentence combining exercises upon several restricted composition tasks. *Journal of Educational Psychology, 62,* 521-525.

Walker, R.L. (1970). The common writer: A case for parallel structure. *College Composition and Communication, 21,* 373-379.

Warriner, J.E., Whitten, M.E., & Griffith, F. (1988). *Warriner's English grammar and composition, Third Course.* New York: Harcourt, Brace, & Jovanovich.

Warriner, J.E., Whitten, M.E., & Griffith, F. (1988). *Warriner's English grammar and composition, Third Course.* Teacher's Edition, Part II. New York: Harcourt, Brace, & Jovanovich.

Waterfall, C.M. (1977). An experimental study of sentence combining as a means of increasing syntactic maturity and writing quality in the compositions of college-aged students enrolled in remedial English classes. Unpublished doctoral dissertation, Utah State University.

Watson, C. (1980). The effects of maturity and discourse type on the written syntax of superior high school seniors and upper level college English majors. Unpublished doctoral dissertation.

Westphal, J. (1991). *Teaching reading comprehension processes* (2'nd Ed.). Englewood Cliffs, NJ: Prentice Hall.

Williams, J.D. (1989). *Preparing to teach writing.* Belmont, CA: Wadsworth Publishing.

Winterowd, W.R. (1975). *Contemporary rhetoric: A conceptual background with readings.* New York: Harcourt, Brace, & Jovanovich.

INDEX

BIOGRAPHICAL SKETCHES OF AUTHORS

Dr. Robert J. Kanellas is the chair of a high school English/Reading department in the suburban north area of Boston, Massachusetts. An educator for 25 years, Dr. Kanellas' research interests have turned to the systematic integration of syntax, content-area reading and expository writing objectives in the Language Arts classroom. As the former director of the Summer Reading Clinic, Dr. Kanellas has implemented this approach at the University of Massachusetts Lowell, where he was recently presented the Coburn Award for excellence in research. He has presented related materials at annual conferences of the New England Reading Association.

Dr. James Carifio is an associate professor of Cognitive Psychology in the College of Education at UMass-Lowell. He has taught English, literature, science, and mathematics in both public and private schools, and has held administrative positions in public higher education and the private sector. Dr. Carifio has published over 100 experimental research studies and has done several national evaluations. His current research interest is complex, real-world human behaviors such as writing, doing geometric proofs, designing experiments, literary criticism, inventing, and formulating policy.

Dr. Lorraine Dagostino is an associate professor of Reading and Language Arts in the College of Education at UMass-Lowell. She has taught English, literature, and reading at the middle school, high school, and college level. Dr. Dagostino recently published *Evaluative Reading and Literacy: A Cognitive View* with Dr. Carifio, which was recently nominated for the University of Louiseville's Grawemeyer Award for significant and important books in Education. Dr. Dagostino's current research interests are critical and evaluative reading and writing.